What people are saying about …

ESSENTIAL ELEMENTS

"I have led men for fifty-one years. I am continually amazed at how many men lack spiritual depth and find themselves living in the misty lowlands of mediocrity. All men long for a cause to die for, a challenge to embrace, and loved ones to protect. The problem is, few men know how to get there. This book should be a primer for every man seeking the heart of God. No one cares what you have to say until they observe how you live. If you live a life of courage, honor, and integrity under the authority of God, people will ultimately want to hear what you have to say, even if they disagree with you. They can dispute your faith or argue about your beliefs. But they cannot dismiss a life well lived in the same direction over time. Vince presents a compelling argument for living a godly life, how to cultivate a meaningful existence that honors the Lord, and how to live a legacy worth leaving in the lives of everyone within your sphere of influence. Unwrapping the Scripture with exceptional clarity, citing supporting examples, providing thought-provoking questions for reflection, and offering helpful suggestions leading to spiritual maturity will help you become a man after God's heart."

Greg Bourgond, DMin, EdD, adjunct professor at University of Northwestern and president and founder of Heart of a Warrior Ministries

"Vince Miller works with men, knows men, speaks to men, and now is writing for men. In this book, *Essential Elements: Forging Godly Men*, Vince uses his own story to provide a road map to better understand what it means to know, follow, and become like Jesus. I can't wait for the next one!"

Steve Sonderman, founder and president of No Regrets Men's Ministry

"Manhood is under attack today. Biblical manhood even more so. Essential Elements is a book that offers men, especially Christian men, the encouragement to be real men of God. Vince Miller is one of the premier leaders in men's ministry today and is eminently qualified to help men find from God's Word what they need to know to truly be men of God. Here is biblical, wise, practical counsel to help you become a godly man, a man's man, and your own man."

Dr. David L. Allen, distinguished professor of preaching, dean of Adrian Rogers Center for Preaching, Mid-America Baptist Theological Seminary

"Biblical manhood is under attack like never before. I'm grateful for a leader and friend like Vince Miller, who is reminding us that godly manhood is rooted in the timeless wisdom of the Bible. Only God's Word and his design can propel us to be the men he has called us to be. Vince has done a masterful job of pointing us to these truths in *Essential Elements*. This book will bless and challenge you!"

Kent Evans, executive director of Manhood Journey and author of *Bring Your Hammer: 28 Tools Dads Can Grab from the Book of Nehemiah*

"I ordered *Essential Elements* thinking it was a vitamin supplement for hair regrowth only to discover it was a book by Vince Miller. However, I was delighted to read the simple and engaging style Vince brings with solid biblical teaching and invitational questions. There is a diagnostic element in this book that helps examine and poke around in areas of a man's heart and mind that normally have 'Do Not Trespass' signs up. Reading and reflecting on this book will make a difference. Don't be stuck."

Bill Arnold, radio host at Faith Radio

"Eternity impacting ministry to men is more than a content dump. This book is more than that. Vince Miller models his Resolute ministry to men with transparency, openness, honesty, and vulnerability. These are the keys to discipling and building godly men—and when we build godly men, everyone wins!"

Brian Doyle, president and founder of Iron Sharpens Iron

"I have known Vince for a couple of decades. It is too trite to say Vince loves the Lord, but he does and he serves him with a passion, dedication, and fervor that is infectious. I really appreciate his love for and devotion to men's ministry as well. Vince enjoys pushing and mentoring men and provides a gifted balance of grace and tough-love guidance that really endears him to men. We all want to go to battle with him. As a speaker and author, he is such a gifted communicator. To God be the glory. He always provides a good mix of light theology and Bible story application, weaving in his life story to make it real, understandable, and applicable. His book *Essential Elements: Forging Godly Men* embodies what makes him such a popular author, teacher, and speaker. This book is yet another Vince Miller resource that is so approachable, usable, and teachable that will facilitate my discipling of men. He finds ways to share Scripture concisely and cogently to inspire the reader. The follow-up questions allow you to engage men in real-world discussion and application to their lives. Thanks, Vince, for another job well done!"

Mark DuVal, JD, FRAPS, president and CEO of DuVal & Associates, PA

"Every man in the church must read this book. Vince delivers a hard-hitting and transformative perspective of manhood founded on God's Word. This is not simply a how-to book for men. The authenticity within these pages will grip the reader and make sense of God's design for men. The truths in this book are personal and profound, and they will guide a man to think and act like God's man."

Dave Mergens, formation pastor of Alexandria Covenant Church

"*Essential Elements* helps men see the misconceptions and lies they believe about what it is to be a man. Relatable stories, challenging questions, and Scripture helped me understand my own story of becoming a man and where my ideas and habits of manhood have been wrong. Vince Miller pointed me back to the ultimate example of a man, Jesus, and how to follow his plan."

Dr. Scott A. Yorkovich, Bible teacher, professor, consultant, and coach

"Vince Miller's *Essential Elements: Forging Godly Men* is the complete package for men all in one book. It lays out perfectly man's problem, God's plan, Jesus as our perfect example, and finally, the process to becoming the men we were meant to be. Vince uses his own story of brokenness to redemption within these pages, making it not only personal, but powerful. I look forward to the next part in this series; you will too."

Todd Harris, director of Men's Ministry at CrossLife Church, Oviedo, FL

"Vince takes the reader through the journey of becoming a man. He illustrates how his grandfather bestowed manhood on him through teaching, modeling, and coaching. He further explains that a man must go to his heavenly Father, God, to find his identity. This is a much-needed book for a society whose currency, in many ways, is lust camouflaged as love. Since lust consumes energy, society is plunging into chaos. To restore order, agape love, real energy, must be injected into society. Finding his identity allows a man to inject love into society, thus returning a measure of order."

Jack Dellinger, PhD, retired BASF Corp site general manager at Enka and Clemson and retired president of Jack Dellinger Enterprises, Inc.

"As an avid reader and someone passionate about personal growth and character development, I wholeheartedly recommend *Essential Elements: Forging Godly Men*. Vince Miller masterfully weaves together timeless wisdom, practical insights, and vast spiritual depth to guide men toward becoming their best selves. In this book, Vince explores the foundational elements that shape godly character—elements like integrity, courage, humility, and perseverance. His biblical references and thought-provoking questions make this book a must-read for any man seeking to grow spiritually and lead a life on mission for God. I strongly encourage readers to dive right in to this latest book from Vince Miller; it's a road map for becoming the man God designed you to be. Live All IN."

Lawrence M. Yurko, EVP at Legacy Sign Group

"I am honored to highly recommend my friend and colleague Vince Miller and his new book. Vince has been a powerful partner in helping to forge the steel and velvet core and character of the thousands of men who are a part of the Leading With Power movement. Vince has been incredibly faithful in keeping his promise to his grandfather to sustain and expand the job that he did in forging Vince's ascent to manhood. You will be well served to access his new work and the many other resources Vince has to offer."

Keith G. Tompkins, cofounder of Leading With Power and husband, father, ironman

"With all the additives that this world requires to define a man, Vince in *Essential Elements* cuts through it all and shows the heart of what God offers for every man, no matter what his background is. He is received and transformed by a loving God who knows him and the man God desires him to be."

Ted Bichsel, associate pastor at Smithtown Gospel Tabernacle, New York

"Vince Miller is a very skilled and Spirit-filled leader. I have known him for approximately four years now, and he's proven to be a great friend and mentor. Vince is continually developing men into becoming spiritual leaders in their homes, workplaces, and communities by mentoring, encouraging, and praying for them not only corporately but also individually. I know men whose lives were changed from connecting with Vince through his mentoring, devotionals, and books such as *Essential Elements: Forging Godly Men*. Vince is a living example of what it is to be a godly man."

Dennis James, Board-certified mental health coach and founder of Restored Spirits Ministries

"With God's help, Vince has done it again with his new book, *Essential Elements: Forging Godly Men*! I have been journeying with Vince since 2016, at which time I began reading his daily devotions, purchasing his books and materials, and even attending one of his men's conferences. In my experiences as a Christ follower, few men have been as successful as Vince in communicating God's uncompromising and life-changing truth as forthrightly and eloquently as he has. His unique method of executing spiritual one-two punches of scriptural truth, and their required personal application, touches the Divine masculinity in men in a way that only God can and desires. If you are in search of a scripturally sound and practically relevant resource that will greatly encourage and empower you toward success in the impending darkness of these times, as well as take you to a new level in your personal walk with Jesus, then I strongly recommend his new book!"

Tom Fredericks, administration and finance director of Every Man a Warrior, Inc.

"Vince is living Hebrews 10:24 as he embodies what it means to spur one another on toward love and good deeds and to be ALL IN and bring God glory by living out our faith authentically and boldly! Vince's special sauce is his ability to hit right at the heart of challenges men face and drive our response as warriors in the fight as Christ followers and kingdom builders. He does the same in this book by digging into some essential lessons we as men need to be reminded of often: we are sinners and require change from within and molded by God's Word; we need to fight to be in God's presence and community; we must repent of our sinful ways and have a clear conscience; and we need to listen intently to God's voice, not others'. This book provides a solid foundation for the full series that I know you will be blessed by. I am a better man for knowing Vince and thank God for his genuine and Spirit-led focus on seeing men live to the fullest that God intended for us on this short time we have here on earth. Live All In!"

John Young, US Army veteran and leader of small groups in multiple churches across the US for over twenty years

"If you are looking for a dangerous book that will challenge and encourage men to repent and really lead like Jesus, then this book is for you! But be warned—it will mess you up in the best way possible! Great job, Vince Miller, on this timely word in a wounded world."

Dave Johnson, pastor at River of Life Church, Elk River, Minnesota

ESSENTIAL ELEMENTS

FORGING GODLY MEN

DAVID C COOK
transforming lives together

ESSENTIAL ELEMENTS
Published by David C Cook
4050 Lee Vance Drive
Colorado Springs, CO 80918 U.S.A.

Integrity Music Limited, a Division of David C Cook
Brighton, East Sussex BN1 2RE, England

DAVID C COOK® and related marks are registered trademarks of David C Cook.

All rights reserved. Except for brief excerpts for review purposes,
no part of this book may be reproduced or used in any form
without written permission from the publisher.

The website addresses recommended throughout this book are offered as a resource to you. These websites are not intended in any way to be or imply an endorsement on the part of David C Cook, nor do we vouch for their content.

Scripture quotations are taken from the ESV® Bible (The Holy Bible, English Standard Version®), copyright © 2001 by Crossway, a publishing ministry of Good News Publishers. Used by permission. All rights reserved. The author has added italics to Scripture quotations for emphasis.

Library of Congress Control Number 2024938432
ISBN 978-0-8307-8713-5
eISBN 978-0-8307-8714-2

© 2024 Vince Miller

The Team: Luke McKinnon, Jeff Gerke, Justin Claypool, Brian Mellema,
James Hershberger, Jack Campbell, Karen Sherry
Cover Design: Micah Kandros

Printed in the United States of America
First Edition 2024

1 2 3 4 5 6 7 8 9 10

060624

To all men who dare to embark on the transformative journey of godly manhood:

The Forged: Godly Men series is dedicated to you. It is a tribute to the courage and resilience you display as you navigate the complex and often challenging path toward becoming the man God has designed you to be.

CHAPTERS

Introduction	13
The Quest of Men	17
The Problem of Men	41
The Only Man	61
The Repentant Man	89
The Man Who Listens	109
The Next Book	141

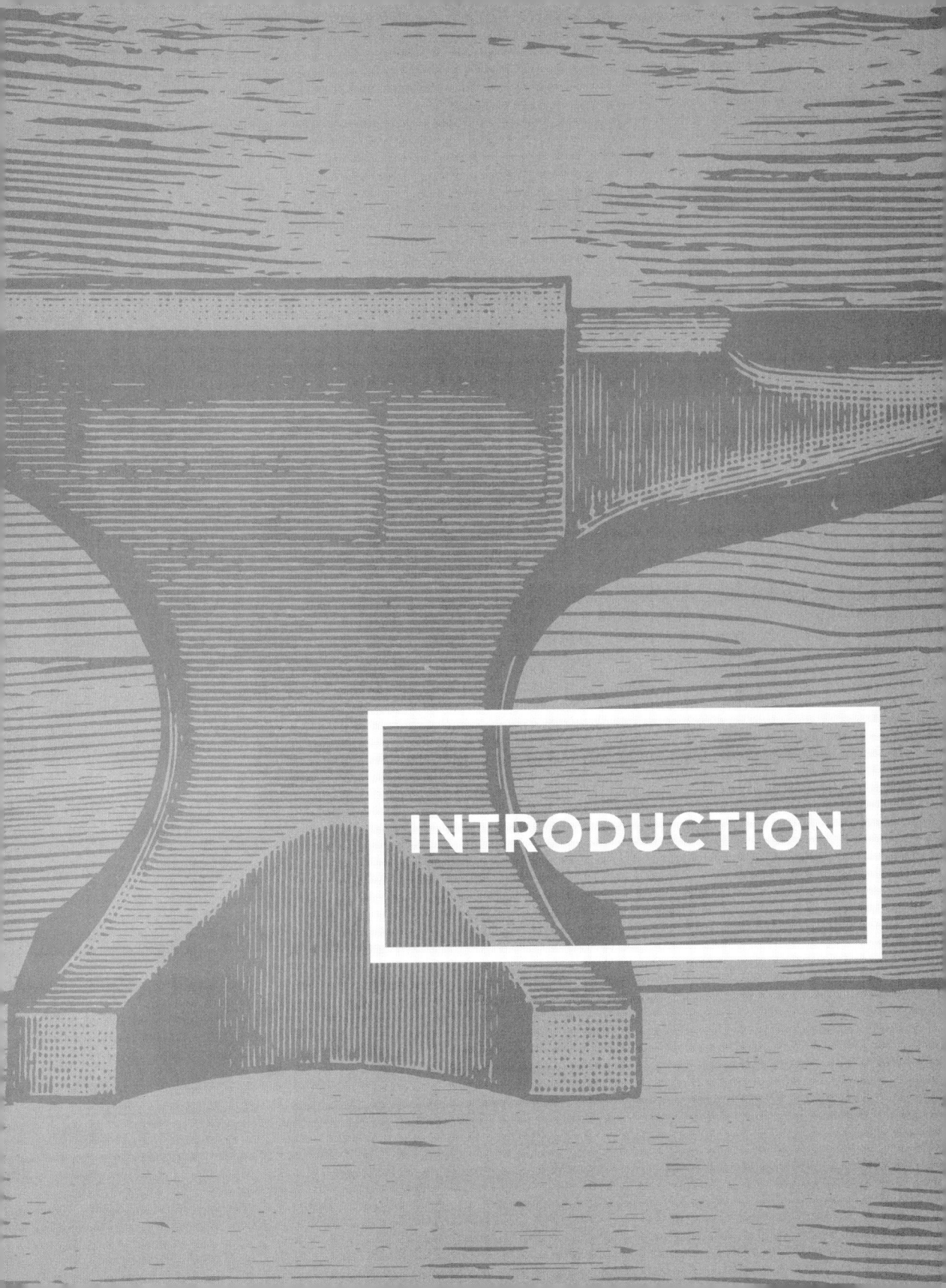
INTRODUCTION

Welcome to a journey that dives deep into the soul of manhood, where certainties blur and doubts loom large. But don't perceive this to be merely another study about men; instead, it's a quest—our exploration into the red-hot forge of biblical manhood.

Here's the driving question for this series: *What makes and defines men?*

Today, the landscape of masculinity is a labyrinth of contradictions. We're hailed as heroes one moment, only to be condemned as zeros the next, all for embodying the same qualities. It's a dizzying whirlwind of expectations and contradictions, leaving men of all ages bewildered and confused.

But I've got some promising news: The essence of genuine manhood is not found in this world, in the latest social media fad, or in pop culture. It's rooted in the timeless wisdom of the Bible. True manhood isn't something we accomplish or earn; it's an ongoing revelation we discover only at the foot of the Cross. But to grasp this truth, we must willingly enter the searing forge of life, where the relentless flames of experience and the divine hand of God meld and shape us into the resilient and purposeful men he has designed us to be.

In the Forged: Godly Men series, we are going to refine three essentials: our understanding of men, our being reforged through discipline, and our sharpening for leadership. All three books are necessary to purify, prepare, and prove ourselves as men.

> **The essence of genuine manhood is rooted in the timeless wisdom of the Bible.**

In the pages of this first book, we won't settle for surface-level answers or temporary solutions. We'll travel back to the very beginning of time, try to figure out where we first stumbled, and identify the issues that trip us up. Most importantly, we'll get to know the divine and perfect man, Jesus, who is the embodiment of authentic manhood. Emulating him is the only way to grasp the true essence of strength and purpose. We'll uncover the impurities of sin and be quenched by the power of true repentance so we can be reformed and reshaped into the image of the one who is forging all men. In the end, our goal is to be remade into God's man—the true man of God.

Throughout this first book, I'll share stories from my own journey and the insights I've gained along the way, connecting them to Scripture. These will reveal one overarching design: the story of a God who melded the first man by his hands from the dust and continues to refine and reshape men like you and me today.

> **Our goal is to be remade into God's man—the true man of God.**

I want this series to be more than just another addition to your shelf; I want it to be a blueprint for crafting a lasting legacy in your life and within your family. So, I urge you to dive into these pages with all your heart. Reflect on the questions posed, commit the scriptures to memory, and engage earnestly in the prayers offered. Through this journey, you'll unlock the profound meaning of being molded by the same divine hand that shapes all men. Together, let's enter the forge on a journey of discovery and transformation, where every page holds the potential to reshape your life for generations to come.

THE QUEST OF MEN

MAN'S PRIMARY QUESTIONS

At the heart of every man's quest for identity and purpose live two profound questions. These questions echo a deeper longing resonating through the corridors of his soul. They are questions that are sweeping in their call yet profoundly personal in their persuasion of men.

What makes a man? And am I that man?

These questions are not mere philosophical musings. They shape the molten core of a man's existence. They silently whisper to him in moments of solitude. They stare back at him from the mirror of his life. They are as old as mankind itself yet relevant to each man walking the earth today.

The first, *What makes a man?* is an attempt to understand the essence of true manhood. It takes him beyond the superficial definitions offered by society, pushing past cultural norms.

The second, *Am I that man?* is even more personal. It's a soul-searching inquiry inviting him to look within. It's about measuring oneself not against the yardstick of mankind, but against the standards of manhood that he has come to know and understand.

As this chapter unfolds, we find ourselves at the edge of a deeper exploration. Here, we will uncover the layers, examine the truths hidden within, and come face to face with answers that are as revealing as they are transformative.

So you know that you are not alone in this journey, here is my story of embarking on the same quest.

BETWEEN TWO HOMES

I vividly recall the moment when these very same two questions confronted me. They were met with a sudden, sharp, and strong yearning to spend more time with my biological dad.

My mother married and divorced twice. She was an attractive and well-known woman, but she had a lingering problem in relationships with men, and she knew it. I was two after her first divorce. She went without a husband for a few years, during which those two questions first hit me. At this point, my response was more practical than philosophical.

In the divorce, my mother gained custody of me, but I was permitted visits with my father every other weekend. He would pick me up on Friday evening and return me to my mother on Sunday evening. I did not know it then, but these weekend visits created a lot of concern for my mother.

My father, unfortunately, didn't fit the mold of a great man, husband, or father. In fact, my childhood counselor called him a sociopath—a diagnosis that was true to form. He was quick to anger, often aggressive, and inflicted verbal abuse without hesitation. His experiences in Vietnam during his military service only exacerbated these issues, plaguing him with haunting nightmares that jolted him awake in terror night after night. Coping with these traumas led him down a path of substance abuse, worsening his already volatile state.

The strain on my parents' relationship was unmistakable, further intensified by my father's emotional turmoil and my mother's inability to cope. Their marriage, already fragile, crumbled within months of his return from war. Neither of them was equipped or emotionally stable enough to sustain a healthy relationship. Eventually, I learned that my father had left for another woman, adding another layer of pain to an already tense and tumultuous situation.

Then fast-forward five years.

I was about eight years old and with my father during a weekend visit when I began to see the glaring differences between my father and mother. At one home, there was a "fun dad" that I visited twice a month. At the other, there was my "overprotective mom," with whom I spent most of my life.

After one of those weekend visits with "fun dad," I insisted on spending more time with my dad. He was virtually uninvolved in every aspect of my life. There were only the weekend visits. Yet the mystery of who he was compelled me to investigate further. Like a curious son, I longed to know more.

We rarely did much together during those weekend visits. My only memories are of occasional games of catch in the backyard. Even then, most of the time, he was busy with other activities that did not involve me. But still the mystery of his life and his masculinity were something I knew I wanted to explore. By nature, as his son, I idolized him, regardless of his character. I aspired to emulate him because of the nature of our relationship.

My mother initially resisted my request, understandably concerned about the implications of my spending more time with my father. Despite her reluctance, I persisted, bringing up the topic not just once, but repeatedly. In the days leading up to the upcoming weekend visit, I pleaded with her to broach the subject with him. Eventually, after much persistence, she relented and promised to address the issue with him upon my return.

As we arrived back home on Sunday evening, I noticed my mother sitting on the porch, lost in thought as she smoked a cigarette. When I stepped out of the car, she motioned for me to wait inside while she had a conversation with my dad. I ran in, dropped my bag, and bolted out the back door toward the side of the house nearest the rear of Dad's truck, trying to catch the whispers of their conversation. This was the first and last time I saw my mother and father together.

She leaned into the passenger window to speak with him. At first, the conversation seemed cordial. Then something changed. Voices escalated. He shouted an accusation at her. She yelled back and then implored him, all to no effect. I am not even sure what they talked about, but I assumed it was me. Then, suddenly, I felt a deep sadness and immense responsibility for even proposing the idea.

Then I heard these words from my father.

"I don't want to spend more time with him. You spend more time with him!"

And then he sped off.

> **What makes a man? Am I that man? And who is the man who will show me the way?**

Needless to say, that visit turned out to be my final one with my dad. Something tragic occurred in that moment, shattering every aspiration I had to emulate him.

Yet the two questions still lingered—*What makes a man? And am I that man?* And now they were complicated by one additional question—*Who is the man who will show me the way?*

REFLECTION AND DISCUSSION QUESTIONS

1. Have you had a moment in your life when you questioned the meaning of manhood? Take a moment to describe what prompted this.

2. How did your childhood experiences and/or your relationships with your parents impact your understanding of manhood and masculinity? Jot down or share how these experiences shaped this understanding.

LOOKING ELSEWHERE FOR ANSWERS

A few years after this event, my mother married again. This was another one of her short-lived marriages. My stepfather was a likable guy, but by this time, my mother's issues were becoming more apparent. Her addictions and personal problems escalated into a violent, nasty divorce.

Soon after the divorce, she realized that her decisions were affecting me, so she promised she would never marry again. And she didn't. But she did have numerous men in and out of the house over the years, which was not a better situation for her or me.

By the time I was thirteen, I was lonely and alone in my quest for manhood. The questions lingered, stirring around in my head. My mother was occupied with other men and work, yet I was desperate for direction. Like most men navigating alone, I turned to my friends for the answers.

Then, this event occurred. It was one that would shape the next few years of my life.

It was in junior high. I was in gym class, clustered with a group of my friends on the basketball court, waiting for class to begin. A friend passing by our class hustled over to us to divulge some of the newest weekend gossip. He was a bit of a bigmouth, so we gathered around him as he gave the weekend update.

He told us news about one of our friends named Tony. His parents had been gone for the weekend, and Tony had invited a girl to spend the weekend at his house. He proceeded to tell us about all the sexual experiences Tony had had with this girl. He spared no detail. If we were all honest, I think every one of us listening was in a bit of shock. But we listened and learned. Then, right as he finished his story, our coach walked in and ushered him out of our class. But as he backed away from our group, he said something I will never forget:

"Well, guys, I guess Tony became a man. Tony became a man!"

As if a thirteen-year-old boy understood what makes a man.

But here's the problem: I believed every word. Right then and there on that basketball court in junior high, I believed that to become a man, I had to penetrate a woman. While this is dead wrong, I believed every word, mainly because a fatherless boy will take direction from anyone who seems to know the answers to the questions that plague us as men: *What makes a man? And am I that man?*

All men are searching for answers to these two questions. Even if we are ashamed to admit it, these questions weigh on our minds. If we don't get answers to them, we will latch on to any answer even if the answers come from the wrong source.

This is precisely why men are so confused about manhood today. We are getting all the wrong information from the wrong sources, which is pointing us in the wrong direction.

REFLECTION AND DISCUSSION QUESTIONS

1. How have peer relationships positively or negatively influenced your understanding of manhood? Try to recall a story like Vince's from your life and the positive or negative idea you picked up from it.

2. As you survey the world today, what do you see as the societal messages that are influencing young men in their beliefs about manhood? Identify who they would hear these from and what these messages might be. What impact might these messages have on these men for years into their future?

THREE POINTLESS PURSUITS

In my years of working closely with men, I've witnessed firsthand the confusion surrounding modern manhood. We're bombarded with misinformation from unreliable sources, guiding us down misguided paths. This confusion is intensified by the fact that men often struggle simultaneously with their pressing questions about life's purpose and meaning. Over my three decades of experience, I've noticed a common trend: when faced with these existential questions, men tend to pursue three seemingly promising paths. However, despite their initial allure, these pursuits often lead to disappointment and confusion, leaving men feeling lost rather than enlightened. Here they are in order of their occurrence.

PURSUIT ONE | REJECTION

This is where some men begin. They begin their pursuit of manhood by rejecting any and all familiar pursuits and proposals. Even though they don't have a good definition of manhood, they know a few things it's not, so they focus their entire pursuit on avoiding those things.

Rejection is their means of self-definition. It's a way for a man to define who he is by separating himself. A man surveys various models of manhood—different behaviors, beliefs, and lifestyles—and then ultimately decides, "That is *not* who I want to be." He rejects former models and hopes that what is left over is what will guide him toward a better version of man. He believes that rejection of perceived negative qualities will result in a better version of himself. Rejection typically manifests itself first in the teen years, when young men start to differentiate themselves by their activities, dress, talk, and friends.

However, rejection alone can be a double-edged sword. While it may initially act as a mechanism for establishing personal boundaries, it can also become a destructive pattern. If a man continually defines his masculinity by what he rejects, he may end up distancing himself from important experiences and valuable relationships. Rejection on its own is a destructive road. If our lives are defined by perpetual rejection, our denials will end up distancing us from everyone and everything. Nothing good lies ahead for the man who persistently proclaims:

- » I don't want to do things your way.
- » I don't believe what you believe.
- » I want to live life my way, not yours.

Jesus illustrated the dangers of rejection in one of his most well-known stories: the Parable of the Prodigal Son.

> There was a man who had two sons. And the younger of them said to his father, "Father, give me the share of property that is coming to me." And he divided his property between them. Not many days later, the younger son gathered all he had and took a journey into a far country, and there he squandered his property in reckless living. (Luke 15:11-13)

In this story, Jesus described a loving and wealthy father with two sons. One day, the younger son came to him and asked for his share of his father's property. This request was like a son angrily telling his father, "I wish you were dead," because, traditionally, a Jewish father would only divide his inheritance among his children just prior to his death. Thus, Jesus portrayed a rebellious son who had chosen to reject his father's way, except for one thing: his father's inheritance—you'll notice he didn't reject that.

In this younger son, we see a man who rejected his father, his way, and his life. So he packed his bags and set out on his way, rejecting his heritage, his teaching, and his religion. This is a textbook example of youthful rejection. Some of you know this younger son well because this was you at one time in life.

This is where many men begin their journey of manhood—outright rejection. They decide to pave their own way by going it alone and casting aside the traditions of their past. Many will initially perceive this pursuit to be noble. The issue with this approach is that it often lacks a clear plan. It starts off undefined because it's only characterized by what it isn't, rather than what it actually is. In his zeal to reject the perceived bad, he might also reject what's good. Ultimately, this overconfidence can spiral into an arrogant march down a road of self-sabotage.

In the parable, the self-sabotage is evident. The younger son rejects his father's ways to "live recklessly." He lives this way because his aim is recklessness. He is consciously rejecting his father's ways while unconsciously sabotaging himself as a man. In choosing a life of rejection, he has inadvertently rejected the only means of becoming a man—surrendering to the Father and his way.

Rejection holds a powerful allure, and it's tempting to pursue. In today's world, there's a concerted effort to steer young men away from traditional biblical principles of manhood. This effort aims to convince them to dismiss these teachings as outdated, privileged, and oppressive relics of the past. Instead, they are encouraged to embrace worldly values and seek validation from society rather than from God. This shift undermines the foundational truths about men found in the Bible, leading many astray from the path of spiritual guidance and wisdom.

> **He is consciously rejecting his father's ways while unconsciously sabotaging himself as a man.**

The current wave of rejection has reached alarming levels in recent years. There's a hostile push to undermine biblical manhood, targeting even the youngest and most vulnerable members of our society. In certain elementary school environments nationwide, traditional teachings on gender and identity are actively rejected. This is no longer a matter of educators inserting their opinions; rejection has become the norm ingrained in the machinery of education.

Educators have taken on a concerning role, actively promoting and pressuring even the youngest and most impressionable individuals to embrace ideologies diametrically opposed to biblical views on gender and identity. These children, who are still developing their faith, are being influenced by trusted authority figures to reject core biblical teachings. They're encouraged to embrace beliefs and behaviors that the Bible identifies as sinful and to adopt genders and identities divergent from biblical and parental guidance. These ideological rejections are portrayed as normal, acceptable, and even desirable, while those who dissent risk facing ridicule from both teachers and friends.

Our rejection of God carries immense consequences. What was formerly deemed an unthinkable rejection of God has now morphed into a widespread and tolerated phenomenon. This rejection is a destructive force, tearing down everything in its wake as we pursue a cultural recklessness. Instead of seeking answers about manhood in and from God, we chase after temporal trends, heed the guidance of godless influencers, and prioritize our own vain pursuits.

But while we may think this is some new phenomenon, let's trace this back. Way back to the first pages of the Bible. Let's reach beyond Jesus's parable to the actual story, one about man and God's indictment on man.

> The LORD saw that the wickedness of man was great in the earth, and that every intention of the thoughts of his heart was only evil continually. (Gen. 6:5)

Rejecting God as our Father and his ways as the way is where all these problems began. Since the beginning, we have rejected the Father's way, trading his way for our way. Much like the first man who wanted to be like God, we, too, want the same—to be like God. We reject the Father, only to inherit an endless number of reckless outcomes. What we fail to realize is that when we reject him as our Father, we have no possible way to be forged into the men and sons we were designed to be.

Rejection is a reckless and pointless pursuit. This path, devoid of reliance on the Father, ultimately leads to self-destruction.

REFLECTION AND DISCUSSION QUESTIONS

1. Which modern ideologies do you feel support biblical views and values, and which ones do you feel reject them? How do these ideologies seek to support or undermine Scripture, godly conduct, and the pursuit of biblical manhood?

2. Reflect on the Parable of the Prodigal Son. How have you experienced the temptation to reject the Father's ways for your own definition and pursuit of manhood? How could such decisions shape your life and faith?

PURSUIT TWO | RITES

The next path men will tread in their quest to define manhood involves what we term the "rite of passage." Throughout history, because many men have sought to prove their manhood down the road of rejection, others have devised ways to counter this trend. Consequently, the rite of passage emerged.

The rite of passage is a means of marking a man's transition from one stage of life to another. Its primary purpose is to instill awareness, instruction, leadership, and cultural continuity in hopes of diverting a man from rejection into acceptance of manhood. The rite, whatever it may be, is a form of social and religious reinforcement for himself and his community. Rites are moments where traditions are passed down, wisdom is communicated, and skills are imparted to prepare a man for the responsibilities and challenges of his next life stage.

Rites of passage have been used repeatedly over millennia. For example, consider the bar mitzvah of Jewish tradition. Or African initiation rituals like the Zulus' *ukuthomba* or the Maasais' *eunoto*. And, of course, there is the Native American vision quest.

Some tend to believe that American culture doesn't practice these rites today. But that's not entirely true. Where there is none, culture constructs them, and though they may be less formal, they do exist. Here are a few:

> **Military Service**—For centuries and across numerous cultures, military service has been a common rite of passage for a young man transitioning into manhood.

> **Graduation**—Completing a declared level of education is another rite for young men.
>
> **Marriage**—Marriage transitions a man from independence to interdependence defining a new relationship with a wife and family.
>
> **Fatherhood**—Becoming a father is a traditional rite of passage that accompanies a name change for men—they become "Dad." It marks a pivotal moment when a man assumes responsibility for nurturing young lives and directing them toward adulthood.

The issue with these rites of passage is that they fall short in transforming boys into men. Men pass through these rites every day, yet still some remain immature. All of us know men who have passed through each one of these stages yet don't act like men. This discrepancy highlights that merely fulfilling these rites doesn't inherently impart manhood. Therefore we have to conclude that culturally constructed rites of passage may serve some purpose but, by themselves, lack the power to cultivate manhood.

In fact, no stage, phase, or rite of passage has ever made a boy into a man. Scripture repeatedly teaches that rites and rituals don't make men. Only God makes men, and men exist by him alone.

> Yet for us there is one God, the Father, from whom are all things and for whom we exist, and one Lord, Jesus Christ, through whom are all things and through whom we exist. (1 Cor. 8:6)

> **No stage, phase, or rite of passage has ever made a boy into a man.**

This draws us back yet again to the fact that there is only one Father. This Father is the one who fathered all things. He gave life to everything, including the first man and thus all men since. Logic and basic reason would suggest that if you want to understand something that has been created, you need to trace that creation back to its creator. In the case of man, the Creator is God.

> Then God said, "Let us make man in our image, after our likeness. And let them have dominion over the fish of the sea and over the birds of the heavens and over the livestock and over all the earth and over every creeping thing that creeps on the earth." (Gen. 1:26)

Man, and his continuity through all humanity, originated by God, not some man-made rite. God is the logical source and means for the making and sustaining of man. Yet every generation believes they have the right rite. Mankind always believes they can invent a better way because they want to play God and be gods. Therefore, by our own rites, we reject the Father. Over millennia, we have invented rites, rituals, and traditions that have become insidious creations. These rites lead men toward arrogance, rebellion, and total destruction. This is why Jesus described the younger son the way he did in the Parable of the Prodigal Son.

> When he had spent everything, a severe famine arose in that country, and he began to be in need. So he went and hired himself out to one of the citizens of that country, who sent him into his fields to feed pigs. And he was longing to be fed with the pods that the pigs ate, and no one gave him anything. (Luke 15:14–16)

This is the result of every man-made rite: self-destructive behavior. One day, we look up to see that we have become the by-product of our self-centered rite. To add insult to injury, we often spiral downward, toiling under the authority of other self-centered, self-made men who oppose our path to manhood. All the

> **We have invented rites and traditions that have become insidious creations. These rites lead men toward arrogance, rebellion, and total destruction.**

while, we long for the comfort of the home of the one Father whose rite we rejected. The Father who generously and graciously imparts identity to all men who surrender to him.

REFLECTION AND DISCUSSION QUESTIONS

1. Reflect on the various cultural rites of passage you have heard of. Which of these do you think best helps boys transition into manhood? Which do you think least helps that transition? Explain how they hurt or help.

2. What is implied in the statement "God is the Father of all mankind"? How does God being the only Father influence your understanding and the rite of becoming a man?

PURSUIT THREE | MERITOCRACY

If we mature beyond rejection and rites on the quest to becoming men, the third pursuit is typically meritocracy. Most men get tripped up with this one for long durations of time. They find it almost impossible to ignore the urge to establish their masculinity on merit and meaning measured by the accumulation of titles, accomplishments, and moral virtue.

Let's face it, we are trained by meritocracy from the day we are born. Meritocracy is the system where our abilities, accomplishments, and achievements become the benchmarks for respect, recognition, and reward. Meritocracy is deeply ingrained into every system of this world. Consider these measurements and their awards:

> **Academic Scholarships**—These are not just monetary gifts; they're votes of confidence in intellect and hard work. Each award is a reward for academic achievement.
> **Educational Certifications**—Every certificate and diploma is a testament to commitment and growth. We don't just do it for the paper; it's an increase in status, salary, and significance in title.
> **Military Decorations**—Military medals are more than decorations on a uniform; they are symbols of sacrifice, courage, in a spirit of service that speaks of our dedication witnessed by others.
> **Sports Achievements**—From public schools to the global stage, every athletic achievement is a story of discipline, physical determination, and athletic excellence rewarding team or individual accomplishments.
> **Artistic Awards**—Whether it's a local gallery feature or an international accolade, artistic awards celebrate personal creativity and ability.
> **Career Accomplishments**—This celebrates milestones of leadership, perseverance, and the impactful application of our gifts. It's focused on our unique contributions to the world.

Awards and rewards like these train us. We are trained by merit from the first time we successfully stand and pee in the toilet to the day we receive that retirement placard. And while merit can be a form of encouragement, something all men need, it can develop in a man a devious way of thinking and a selfish, insidious drive that forms his identity.

So many men get caught in the trap of meritocracy. It happens all the time, and men are driven by it. This is because merit is powerful. It feeds our selfish tendencies. When merit is received without spiritual discretion, a man's pride will feast on the praise until it becomes the basis of his identity.

Men who are fixated on the pursuit of meritocracy operate under the belief that their worth hinges on their achievements and accomplishments. They pour countless resources into striving for the next accolade or reward, often making significant sacrifices along the way. This might mean sacrificing time, energy, money, and effort, sometimes at the expense of their relationships at home with their wife and children. Even more concerning is their tendency to eventually compromise their moral and spiritual values in pursuit of their goals. While they may perceive their pursuit as noble, they fail to recognize that their relentless pursuit of meritocracy is controlling them.

> When merit is received without spiritual discretion, a man's pride will feast on the praise until it becomes the basis of his identity.

A man can become so engulfed in the pursuit of merit that his thoughts revolve solely around titles, achievements, and moral virtue. In this relentless chase, he grows distant from his family and God, justifying his pursuit as the means of their only provision. Trapped in the cycle of meritocracy, he loses sight of the one and only Provider, God, and he becomes the sole provider of his own provision.

The harsh reality of this pursuit hits home when a man is terminated from his work. For someone whose identity is deeply intertwined with his career and status, termination is the collapse of his world because it was the basis of his identity. Without provision this man can no longer provide; therefore, he is left to wonder who he is. Stripped of the job and title that once provided his worth, he confronts the emptiness of the third pursuit. It's a sobering realization because a man who built his life on the principles of meritocracy finds himself without merit. In many instances, he struggles with feelings of aimlessness and insecurity because he has relied too heavily on merit for his validation.

Even believing men can fall prey to a religious version of meritocracy, a phenomenon so widespread in the church that it has its own name—"works-based righteousness." It's the notion that you can earn favor from God, securing eternal rewards through your own efforts. But this mindset ignores a fundamental truth: all men are sinners deserving only God's wrath.

Spiritually, our merit counts for nothing; it's meritless. The only merit that holds weight and value is that of Jesus and his righteousness. Works-based righteousness is merely meritocracy with a moral or godly disguise.

Let's revisit the Parable of the Prodigal Son, and you'll see this version of meritocracy embodied in the other son—the older brother.

> Now [the father's] older son was in the field, and as he came and drew near to the house, he heard music and dancing. And he called one of the servants and asked what these things meant. And he said to him, "Your brother has come, and your father has killed the fattened calf, because he has received him back safe and sound." But he was angry and refused to go in. His father came out and entreated him, but he answered his father, "Look, these many years I have served you, and I never disobeyed your command, yet you never gave me a young goat, that I might celebrate with my friends. But when this son of yours came, who has devoured your property with prostitutes, you killed the fattened calf for him!" (Luke 15:25–30)

The older son's anger and self-righteousness reveal his underlying motives. Though the story isn't explicitly about masculinity, we can definitely view the older son's journey as a quest for manhood by self-righteous merit—a concept parallel to works-based righteousness. Notice how Jesus described him:

- » In the field, busy with work.
- » Angered at his brother's reception.
- » Defending the many years he had served.
- » Refusing to call his brother by name, enter his father's home, or celebrate with him.
- » Rejecting his father's decision to extend grace and forgiveness to his brother.

Why did Jesus describe him this way?

Because the older son believed that righteous merit and moral virtue made him his father's man—or that, at a minimum, they would make him an acceptable son. He was so overcome by his moral merit that he assumed his father would act based on this same meritocracy. He even demanded that his father should. But this father was not deterred, because he was not just any father—he was the Father of all.

> **And [the father] said to him, "Son, you are always with me, and all that is mine is yours. It was fitting to celebrate and be glad, for this your brother was dead, and is alive; he was lost, and is found." (Luke 15:31-32)**

In the end, the older son, though he looked to be morally good and deserving of merit, made a tragic presumption. Contrary to the rejection of the younger son, the older son assumed that his hard work would earn him the right to his standing and inheritance. Yet we discover this was never the case. His beliefs had been so corrupted by his pursuit of meritocracy that he could not make sense of his father's generosity in giving out rewards where merit had not been earned. So he stood outside the celebration in disbelief, feeling bitter, angry, and confused. Ironically, if we trace the origins of this parable back to why Jesus told it, we'll discover that it stemmed from the self-righteous grumbling of the scribes and Pharisees, whose merit-based mindset was casting judgment on self-centered sons who had come home (Luke 15:1–2).

Meritocracy, whether in spiritual or secular contexts, is a path frequently chosen by men in their quest for self-validation. Whether shaped by societal pressures or religious doctrines, they're indoctrinated with the notion that amassing titles, accomplishments, and moral virtues will ultimately define their manhood. Yet this journey inevitably leads to a dead end—a realization that the pursuit of external validation can never truly fulfill the longing within.

REFLECTION AND DISCUSSION QUESTIONS

1. Reflect on how the pursuit of titles, accomplishments, and moral virtue can lead a man away from godly manhood. How have you seen this play out in your life or in the lives of others?

2. Think about the impact of meritocracy on a man's identity and sense of self-worth. How does this system shape a man's understanding of success and achievement and even his understanding of himself and God?

MANHOOD REDISCOVERED

With the parable, it is clear that both men were desperately confused in one of three ways. The younger, self-centered son chose paths of rejection and man-made rites. The older, self-righteous son chose the path of meritocracy. In the story, Jesus speaks to both kinds of men and their respective pursuits. He wants them to know that it's not rejection, man-made rites, or merit that establishes a man, but a loving Father, God, who graciously and generously imparts identity to any son who wants to come home.

In the story, the father exemplifies God, the ultimate Creator and Redeemer of men. He graciously welcomes back any son who repents, turning away from his futile ways. In the coming chapter titled "The Repentant Man," we'll explore repentance further, but for now, notice how the father responded to the repentant son in the parable:

> **It's not rejection, man-made rites, or merit that establishes a man, but a loving Father, God, who graciously and generously imparts identity to any son who wants to come home.**

> The father said to his servants, "Bring quickly the best robe, and put it on him, and put a ring on his hand, and shoes on his feet. And bring the fattened calf and kill it, and let us eat and celebrate. For this my son was dead, and is alive again; he was lost, and is found." And they began to celebrate. (Luke 15:22-24)

The father restored to his son what he had previously rejected. He restored his identity by lavishing him with symbols of belonging: a robe, a ring, shoes, and the grandest of meals. While the son refused these former symbols, he could not restore them. These tokens couldn't be replicated by rites, rituals, or earned through merit; they had to be freely given and restored by the father.

This is where manhood begins—with the Father. God alone made men; therefore, he is the only one who could ever remake them.

Our entire existence revolves around the Father. For repentant men, his greatest gift is the boundless riches of a restored relationship with him. However, to receive his relationship and all his blessings, we must abandon all other pursuits and return to the one whose merit truly matters.

All this brings us to the end of all our pursuits and to a far more relevant question in our quest for manhood. Instead of asking, *What makes a man? And am I that man?* the more relevant question is, *Who makes men?* This subtle shift in the focus of our questions inevitably leads us to a righteous pursuit. We naturally veer from notions of rejection, rites of passage, and merit-based systems. Like the Prodigal Son, we find ourselves compelled to return home confronting the undeniable truth: submitting to the Father is fundamental to becoming a son and his man.

Are you ready to surrender and return to the Father who welcomes lost men home?

> Instead of asking, *What makes a man? And am I that man?* the more relevant question is, *Who makes men?*

Father,

Thank you for your boundless love, forgiveness, and generosity. I surrender completely to you, acknowledging you as the ultimate Creator and Restorer of men. I turn from my rejection, rites, and meritocracy and am ready to return to you, finding my identity and purpose in your embrace. Establish me as your son, in your home, with your riches, as your man.

In Jesus's name, amen.

REFLECTION AND DISCUSSION QUESTIONS

1. In what ways do you, like the two sons, seek to establish your own identity through rejection, rites, or merit? How does surrendering to the Father's loving authority challenge or change your understanding of true manhood?

2. The story illustrates a powerful moment of repentance and restoration. Reflect on a time in your life when you made a similar "return to the Father." How did this experience reshape your understanding of your identity and purpose as a man?

THE PROBLEM OF MEN

THE STAIN OF SIN

Years ago, while living in Texas, I embarked on a DIY project on a sweltering summer day. The project? Laying limestone pavers for a backyard patio. While I labored under the blazing sun, my wife and three children hung out inside our air-conditioned home, occasionally venturing out to gauge my progress beneath the relentless heat.

As the temperatures rose into the high nineties, my thoughtful wife periodically placed large glasses of ice-cold red Gatorade by the door to quench my thirst.

Drawing close to the end of the day, and focused on finishing my task, I decided to hold off on that last glass. It stood there, ice-filled, as a promising reward. But when I finally finished my work and walked toward my drink, I saw, to my astonishment, that it had vanished. I initially thought, *Is it that hot out here?* That was until I spotted my five-year-old son playing in the driveway.

I called him over and, in amusement, asked him, "Did you drink my Gatorade?"

He quickly replied, "No."

I pointed to the empty glass and inquired again, "Did you drink my red Gatorade that was in this glass?"

He replied confidently, "No, Dad!"

Trying to hold back a smile, I looked at him again and asked, "Are you sure?"

His bright eyes stared back and in a serious tone he said, "No, Dad, I didn't drink it."

I burst into laughter and sent him back into the house.

What made the moment so laughable was the bright-red Gatorade mustache on his face and his freshly stained red tongue. He had overlooked the undeniable evidence. He had shamelessly relished every drop of my ice-cold reward.

This is man's nature. It is exposed even in a young boy. Man is undeniably stained by our acts of sin and unwillingness to accept it.

REFLECTION AND DISCUSSION QUESTIONS

1. The evidence of the son's action is visibly clear, yet he denies it. Reflect on a time when you tried to hide a mistake or a sin, thinking it was concealed but realizing later it was entirely evident to everyone else. How did this experience impact your understanding of honesty and transparency in your spiritual journey?

2. The son's red stain can serve as a metaphor for how sin can be clearly seen in our lives, even when we attempt to deny or hide it. What steps can you take to address sin and find accountability on your path to spiritual growth?

THE GENESIS OF SIN'S STAIN

To comprehend humanity's sinful nature and the mark of our transgressions, we must trace it back to its origins. Nearly everything you need to understand about sin is captured in the initial narrative of Genesis 3. This story, chronicling the first man, the first woman, and the inception of sin, is essential reading for all men and should be revisited repeatedly throughout our lives.

But before we get too far ahead, let's make sure we understand the meaning of the word *sin*.

Sin is an ancient biblical term. The Old and New Testaments have different words for sin. At its core, sin denotes a condition of guilt or actions that deviate from righteousness. Yet its simplest definition is "to miss the mark" or "to fall short of the goal." In Genesis 2–3, we witness how God established a standard for the first man and woman, only for them to fall short of meeting it.

> And the LORD God commanded the man, saying, "You may surely eat of every tree of the garden, but of the tree of the knowledge of good and evil you shall not eat, for in the day that you eat of it you shall surely die." (Gen. 2:16-17)

God granted man incredible freedom. He allowed him to eat freely from the trees in the garden, even from the Tree of Life, which provided eternal life (Gen. 2:9). However, by divine decree, one tree was forbidden—the Tree of the Knowledge of Good and Evil. In this, God established a single boundary for man. He set a target with a lone limit.

Yet man and woman defied this one rule. They "missed the mark" of obedience to God's command. This is the first occurrence of human sin. And from it we gain two insights into the nature of sin.

FIRST | SIN IS AN OFFENSE AGAINST GOD

We discover first that sin is a choice to turn away from the person and authority of God. This rejection stems from the desire to live independent from the Father. The temptation by the serpent makes the seminal desire evident: man and woman wanted to be "like God." This willful desire was a rejection of God's authority. It introduces a break between us and God, creating a barrier of sin and destroying harmony in the relationship.

SECOND | SIN IS MORE THAN A MISTAKE

Second, sin isn't a minor error or oversight. It's more consequential. Sin is rebellion against the rule of God. It isn't something God takes lightly, so we shouldn't take it lightly either. Sin isn't a slipup or mistake—this is categorically wrong. It's a deliberate decision to break his divine decree. Sin is a breach of obedience to God, intentional defiance of God's will, prioritizing our will above his, which puts us directly in the path of his judgment and wrath.

So here is a fuller definition of *sin* based on the two insights above:

Sin is to miss the mark set by God. It isn't just a mistake. It's a conscious act of willful disobedience to God stirred by a desire to be like him. Sin separates us from a relationship with God and demands punishment by a righteous God.

This definition should be enough to incite a divine dread in men. But it's usually not until we see the seismic effects of sin that we understand how dreadful its impact is.

> **Sin is to miss the mark set by God. It isn't just a mistake. It's a conscious act of willful disobedience to God stirred by a desire to be like him.**

REFLECTION AND DISCUSSION QUESTIONS

1. Reflect on a time when you have "missed the mark" in your own life. How did this experience help you understand the deeper nature of sin as more than a mistake but as a deliberate departure from God's way?

2. Considering the definition of sin as a conscious act of rebellion against God, how do you see this manifesting in your daily life? Reflect on moments when you might have prioritized your desires over God's commandments. What are the subtle ways in which you might be missing the mark in obedience to God?

Sin's Seismic Effects

In 1989, while living in the San Francisco Bay Area, I experienced the Loma Prieta earthquake, a devastating 6.9 magnitude quake. On the evening of October 17, during the renowned Bay Bridge World Series (a battle between the San Francisco Giants and the Oakland Athletics), it hit. The quake created widespread chaos. Key landmarks like the San Francisco–Oakland Bay Bridge and the Cypress Street Viaduct in Oakland were shattered. The picturesque Marina District in San Francisco was greatly damaged.

When the earthquake struck, I was a little late on my way to a friend's house to watch the third game of the World Series. As I approached my car, the ground began to shake. Having grown up in the Bay Area, I had been through many quakes before, but this one was unmatched.

The sight was chilling to behold. I witnessed the sheer force of the earthquake as it turned the earth into liquid. It looked like a massive rock had been plunged into a pond, causing catastrophic ripples through solid concrete. You could literally see the waves ripple through buildings and roads as if they were floating on the surface of the water. Buildings, roads, and bridges crumbled, even miles from the epicenter. This disaster claimed sixty-three lives and wounded countless other people, leaving an indelible mark on the region's psyche and history.

The Loma Prieta earthquake powerfully illustrates the aftermath of sin: a singular event with far-reaching ripples. The epicenter of all sin is found in a single occurrence in Genesis 3: "She took of its fruit and ate, and she also gave some to her husband who was with her, and he ate" (v. 6).

But the event of sin was not an isolated event. Its aftershocks were not confined to the Garden and to the first man and woman. Their choices—and the consequences of their sin—were profound. It was a sinful quake with immoral ripples felt across time. It was one act of sin with two sinful effects: an initial effect with a ripple effect.

The Initial Effect

Sin's first effect, like a rock plopped into calm water, may initially appear inconsequential. The stone makes only a splash and then sinks into the deep.

In the Garden, the woman didn't impulsively grab the forbidden fruit, accidentally or mindlessly pluck it. It was a willful, intentional, and purposeful act of selfishness. First, its appeal ensnared her. Second, she rationalized the choice. Finally, she "took … and ate" (Gen. 3:6). Right there is the epicenter of the quake of sin—the seminal bite that has rebelliously rocked mankind ever since.

This was sin's first effect. Yet there was a second, and it was far more destructive.

The Ripple Effect

Once the woman had broken God's decree, she advanced the ripple of her sin by handing the fruit to her husband. The first man was there as well, and he also ate. Eve's disobedience wasn't an isolated event or a single, stand-alone sin. It had a cascading effect. This was the ripple of sin propelling outward, and its wake had substantial force.

THE PROBLEM OF MEN

The same is true in our lives. Sin has both an initial effect and a ripple effect. Sin's effects are never singular. Each sin has sinful swells coming from aftershocks felt by those near and far. Often, these reach across generations. In the case of the first sin, we still feel the swells even today.

Here is how Paul stated this truth:

> **Therefore, just as sin came into the world through one man, and death through sin, and so death spread to all men because all sinned. (Rom. 5:12)**

Sin has both a seminal and surging effect that swells and spills into future generations. This means the problem of our sin cannot be remedied by merely correcting a single bad behavior or action, even though that is worth addressing. Sin has a catastrophic, ongoing effect because disobedience to God affects everything and everyone. These issues extend far beyond us, hurting others we did not intend to harm. Like the Loma Prieta earthquake, the initial event was bad, but the aftershocks were far more costly.

But most men overlook both of these effects. When they sin, their focus is solely on that fleeting moment of pleasure. Sin will offer temporary gratification, which is why we're drawn to it. However, most men fail to look beyond this pleasure to the far-reaching consequences and repercussions of their actions. They fail to pause and reflect on the ripples of repercussions that sins, like adultery, will trigger. The ripple effects include spiritual turmoil, shattered trust, emotional scars, guilt, shame, hurt children, social isolation, tarnished reputations, job loss, divorce proceedings, legal expenses, and much more. Let's also not overlook the impact on another entire family, who also experiences all these ripples. Sin is never an

> **Sin has a catastrophic, ongoing effect because disobedience to God affects everything and everyone.**

isolated event; it involves people, and its consequences send out wakes and waves of relentless destruction.

Unfortunately, most men discover the meaning of sin, its offense, and its effects the hard way—by disobeying God. I wish we didn't always have to learn the hard way, but sometimes it's the only way to acknowledge that there's much more at play.

REFLECTION AND DISCUSSION QUESTIONS

1. Why do men have a hard time thinking through the ripple effects of sin before they act? Would knowing the potential effects ahead of time change the way men respond to decisions to sin?

2. Reflect on a moment in your life when a seemingly small choice led to significant consequences. Describe how this event rippled out to impact not only your life but also the lives of those around you. Share how this event and the lessons of your sin deepened your understanding of sin's far-reaching effects.

FIVE SYMPTOMATIC SINS

Despite the harsh realities sin presents, there is wisdom to be gleaned from our sin for those open to its teachings. These lessons, though challenging, unveil a discernible pattern, offering insight into the symptoms and root causes of the struggles faced by men.

A few years back, I put a link at the top of my website that read, "Need Prayer?" It's still there today. Once I put it up, I quickly learned that men want and need prayer. Men were always writing me emails asking for prayer, so I decided to make it more inviting for them.

As I anticipated, the requests poured in. At first, I was the only one responding. Over time, the response became overwhelming. Therefore, we developed a volunteer team to help pray for these men. Today, this has become a sizable online prayer ministry to men.

Through this prayer ministry, I stumbled upon an unexpected revelation about men: their requests consistently circled around five primary concerns. Through numerous requests, it became unmistakably clear that men consistently seek support for these five areas. These requests reverberate our most pervasive sins. Presented next, in descending rank, are the recurring themes and common struggles faced by men.

ONE | MARITAL ISSUES

Marriage is at the top of the list. For men, marriage is far more important than they let on. They usually don't realize how much they care about it until issues arise. The challenges they face range from communication breakdowns resulting in resentment to issues of sexual intimacy and infidelity that have eroded trust. Some men struggle with power dynamics in the home, disrespect, or various stressors like finances, family, and health. Many of these problems fly under the radar until they intensify. Overwhelmed, men ask for prayer, hoping it will provide the solution they simply cannot find.

TWO | FINANCIAL ISSUES

Financial difficulties rank second. Factors include job loss, unanticipated expenses, poor financial decisions, addictions, or legal problems. Some men struggle because they have never been financially responsible. Others stagger under the weight of unexpected expenses that have put pressure on them and their families. Finding themselves trapped behind mountains of debt, they seek prayer, hoping for a divine way of escape.

THREE | COMPULSION ISSUES

Addiction is a recurring prayer request from men. These addictions can range from substance abuse to behavioral compulsions like gambling or pornography. Many men wrestle silently with these issues, feeling isolated, ashamed, or unequipped to break free on their own. Overwhelmed by the burden of their struggles and the harm they've inflicted on themselves and others, they turn to prayer, seeking strength, hope, and healing.

FOUR | HEALTH ISSUES

Health concerns are a frequent topic of prayer for men. Many are facing a new diagnosis, managing chronic illnesses, or confronting the vulnerabilities of aging. They often struggle with fear and uncertainty and the repercussions these issues can have on their roles as providers or protectors. Health challenges can also stir more profound reflections about mortality and purpose. Feeling helpless or anxious about the future and desiring healing, strength, or peace, they turn to prayer for support, solace, and hope.

FIVE | CAREER ISSUES

Concerns about career and calling drive men to seek prayer. Navigating professional challenges, facing job loss, or feeling unfulfilled in their chosen path can lead to profound questions about their identity and value. The pressures to succeed, provide for families, and find meaning in their work can become overwhelming. Many men question whether

THE PROBLEM OF MEN

they're on the right path or are meeting their responsibilities adequately. Desiring clarity, direction, and affirmation of their purpose, they turn to prayer, hoping to find alignment with their divine calling.

That's about it. Five in all. Occasionally, some one-off issues will come up, but this list summarizes and ranks what most men are thinking and seeking prayer about.

But here's the unexpected lesson I learned from hearing all the prayer requests of men: most men don't want to be changed; they mostly want God to change their situation.

Let me clarify.

The men who write to us want us to pray to God on their behalf, which is the right impulse and a great place to begin. Men should seek God when they are in despair, and men need other men to pray for them. But often, buried in their requests, are hints of a great misunderstanding about their sin. What they want is for God to fix the messy effects of their sin but not the issue that caused the sin in the first place. What they want is a divine pass on the impact and effects of their sin.

What began as a tiny pebble of corruption has now become an insurmountable mountain of sin. They are daunted by the work it would take to address all the issues, so they conclude that the quickest way to resolve the matter is to ask a righteous man to pray to God on their behalf to remove the mountain of consequences.

> **Most men don't want to be changed; they mostly want God to change their situation.**

Many of these men come to us exhausted; in desperation, they want us to pray for their situation, asking God to remove the sin, its ripples, and the damage to all the people who have been hurt in the process.

And mind you, we love praying for these men. They are broken and need divine intervention. But they usually want only a change to their circumstances and not to be changed because they are so absorbed by the consequences of their circumstances.

In fact, among all the prayer requests we receive, requests for personal change are exceedingly rare. So rare, in fact, that when a man does make such a request, it catches me off guard. It evokes a profound emotional response because it reveals a man who is prepared and eager to

> **Men usually want only a change to their circumstances and not to be changed because they are so absorbed by the consequences of their circumstances.**

> **A change to our circumstances changes nothing.**

surrender and be totally changed. Often weary and worn out from attempting to rectify his circumstances and even praying for his circumstances, he recognizes that the root of the issue lies within himself. He is ready to relinquish control to God. This is a man who comprehends that the solution doesn't lie in changing his circumstances but in being changed himself.

With this, we have traced the symptoms back to the core problem. Men don't just have a sin problem; they are sinful to the core. This is why we sin and why we experience the effects of sin. A change to our circumstances changes nothing. It's the man who must be changed, and most men never stop to consider this.

But now that we've pinpointed the core issue, it's time to cease all efforts to merely address the symptoms of sin and instead focus on addressing the core problem: the presence of sin within man.

REFLECTION AND DISCUSSION QUESTIONS

1. Consider a time when you faced a challenging situation. Reflect on whether your desire was more focused on alleviating the consequences or on addressing the underlying sin or character flaw that might have contributed to it. How might redirecting your focus to the root cause of your struggles lead to more profound spiritual growth and transformation?

2. Given the rarity of men asking for prayer for personal change, how can you actively incorporate this aspect into your own prayer life? Reflect on an area of your life where you recognize the need for personal growth or transformation. How can you courageously pray not just for a change in circumstances but also for a change in yourself, aligning more closely with God's will and character?

FOUR TRUTHS THAT LEAD TO A SOLUTION

One thread runs throughout human history: sin has a catastrophic impact on all mankind. We read headlines about it daily because an inherited bent toward sin lies at the core of every man's heart. This inclination has destroyed empires, broken relationships, and darkened our souls. From the days of Adam till today, we have a problem not only with what we do but with who we are.

This problem is so big that most people don't even like to talk about it. But if we understand the following four biblical truths, we will uncover the good news.

TRUTH ONE | SIN AFFECTS ALL MANKIND

> Therefore, just as sin came into the world through one man, and death through sin, and so death spread to all men because all sinned. (Rom. 5:12)

This verse explains that the very first wrongful thought, desire, and action that man committed, way back in the Garden, created a wake of destruction that has continued to sweep across mankind to today. That first disobedience set in motion a subsequent chain of quakes, tremors, tsunamis, and aftershocks. It has impacted every man in every generation. No man is exempt from this wake, and that's the biblical truth.

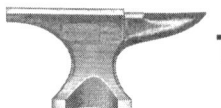

TRUTH TWO | SIN EARNS MAN A WAGE

> For the wages of sin is death. (Rom. 6:23)

Next, we discover that sin has wages. In daily life, wages are what we earn for our work. They are the deserved payment for our labor; it's a straightforward transaction. In this verse, our sin is likened to a form of labor, and the wage it pays out is death. This is not only a physical death but also a spiritual death—a separation from God, the source of life and goodness. The transaction makes sin the most deceptive wage you have ever worked for. It promises pleasure but pays out death. The payout is always accruing and eventually inevitable, and in the end, we will be due for what we have done.

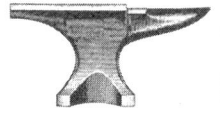

TRUTH THREE | THE WAGE OF SIN MUST BE PAID

> [Jesus] is the propitiation for our sins, and not for ours only but also for the sins of the whole world. (1 John 2:2)

Because the wages for our sins were accruing God's wrath, something had to be done. God's wrath had to be satisfied. The only payment God would accept was atonement by blood from a righteous and sinless man. There was only one of those in history. Jesus, the Son of Man, is the one who paid sin's debt with his perfect, righteous, and holy life. His life's wage was perfect. His gift was immense. He paid a debt that you and I could never afford.

TRUTH FOUR | JESUS SAVES MEN FROM SIN

> For God so loved the world, that he gave his only Son, that whoever believes in him should not perish but have eternal life. (John 3:16)

Across the reaches of time, there echoes a final truth: We cannot save ourselves. We need saving. It's the only possible way to avoid the aftermath of our sins. The magnitude of sin's wake and wages is too great. We need to be saved by a Savior of unparalleled resources, might, and grace.

Then enters Jesus.

The Savior who saves, the one who paid our sin debt with his blood, shattering the chains of death and gifting us eternal life through his resurrected life.

The way to freedom, life, and eternity is both simple and profound: *believe*. That's it. It is too good to be true, but the Father is rich, and his Son paved and paid the way. It's not by rejection, rite, or acts of meritocracy. It's paid by him for you because he loves you.

But it gets even better.

As you sit reading this chapter, you can break free from sin, spiritual death, and God's wrath to receive eternal life. If you are weary and burdened by sin's weight, wake, and wages, it can all be lifted at this very moment. All you need to do is go all in for him who went all in for you. Place your unwavering trust in him. Believe wholeheartedly in those four truths and leave behind the bondage and burden of your sin. Surrender to Jesus and accept him as your Savior and Lord. Jesus is the means, rite, and way for you to become the man God intended you to be. And if you are ready to take this step in becoming a man of God, here is a short prayer you can pray to mark this moment if you're ready:

> **Across the reaches of time, there echoes a final truth: We cannot save ourselves. We need saving.**

Father,

When I survey my life and choices, I see a pattern of sin. I sin repeatedly. I have tried fixing it and making things right, but I realize I can't because it's me that's broken. I am not asking you to fix my situation but to fix me. Take my wretched life, broken and infested with sin.

Jesus, I believe you lived, died, and rose again. You alone paid my debt for the wages of all my sins. I believe you paid them with the blood sacrifice of your holy life for me on the Cross. You rose again in victory over physical and spiritual death and made the payment for the wages of my sin. I believe this and receive this gift now. Change me to the core, give me a new heart and new desires, and may your Holy Spirit live forever in me.

In Jesus's name, I pray. Amen.

REFLECTION AND DISCUSSION QUESTIONS

1. Did you pray the prayer above? If so, tell someone immediately. Find a believer and ask him to help you take some first steps in your newfound life of surrender to Jesus.

2. Considering the truth that "sin affects all men" and the idea that it's not just about what we do but who we are, reflect on how this inherited bent toward sin has manifested in your own life. How has it influenced your thoughts, actions, and relationships? What specific instances come to mind when you have seen the impact of this inherent nature?

3. Since Jesus paid the debt for your sins and offered you salvation, how should this influence your daily choices and attitudes? What does believing in Jesus as your Savior mean for you in terms of how you live your life, confront sin, and engage with others? What areas in your life do you need to trust in the transformative power of Jesus's sacrifice more fully?

THE ONLY MAN

DIRECTION FROM A GODLY MAN

When I was about fifteen, soon after my mother's second divorce, my grandfather came over to our house one day. Because his visit was so out of the ordinary, I secretly listened to my mother talking with him down the hall.

They sat at the kitchen table, and their topic of discussion was me.

It was a surprising and heartwarming dialogue. I listened as my grandfather implored my mother to allow me to come live with him and my grandmother for a while. It was evident to us all that my mother was struggling emotionally. After the discussion, they reached an agreement that having a stable male presence in my life was crucial. Shortly thereafter, I moved into my grandparents' home.

My grandfather was a tough veteran who was molded by farm life and seasoned by years of military service. His disciplined approach to life left an impression on everyone around him. Meanwhile, my grandmother, also from a farming lifestyle, spent years running her own small diner, whipping up meals at the drop of a hat. Now in the latter part of their lives, they found themselves with plenty of time to pour their wisdom and love into shaping my life.

Life was much different in their home. To begin with, meals were not at all what I was used to. They had a modest military-style home with a small kitchen and eating area. Four chairs sat around their small round dining table. One seat was dedicated to my grandfather, another was for my grandmother, and one of the other two was left for me.

I remember that first dinner in their home. I came to the table as my grandfather clarified where I could sit. Then Grandma began placing the food on the table. As she did, I instinctively reached out for one of the plates.

My grandfather reached over abruptly and slapped the top of my hand. "At our home," he said sternly, "we wait until your grandmother has served the entire meal."

> This wasn't just a meal—it was a discipleship experience. He was training me to think and act differently and using mealtime as his teaching tool.

As instructed, I sat with my hands on my lap and waited as she presented the meal. She made numerous trips back and forth from the kitchen. Each time she prepared a protein, starch, and vegetable.

As soon as she set the last plate down, I reached instinctively for the meat.

My grandfather slapped my hand again explaining, "In our home, we wait until your grandmother has joined us at the table."

I began to understand that this wasn't just a meal—it was a discipleship experience. He was training me to think and act differently and using mealtime as his teaching tool.

My grandmother finally untied her cooking apron and sat down to join us. I looked to my grandfather for approval before reaching for the food.

With a stern look, he said, "Before we eat, we pray for the meal. Bow your head and close your eyes." Then he prayed a short but on-point prayer. However, I didn't bow my head and close my eyes. I just watched and listened because I was mesmerized.

At his "Amen," they raised their heads and opened their eyes. Grabbing their napkins, which sat neatly on their plates, he said, "Next time we pray, I want you to bow your head, close your eyes, and give respect to God."

I nodded in agreement, unsure how he knew I had not submitted to his request. But I didn't want to get my hand slapped again, so next time, I did comply.

To say the least, Grandma's food was awesome. I never really had a meal like this at my mother's home. Most of the time, I ate alone and heated some pizza rolls or a microwavable dinner, but nothing home-cooked. The food was so good that I ate pretty fast. Much faster than my grandparents ate.

After I crammed in that last bite, I set my fork down and mistakenly thought I could leave. I started to stand up, but as I did, my grandfather grabbed the corner of my shirt and pulled me back into my seat.

He explained, "At our house, we sit together at the table until your grandmother is finished."

My grandma ate slowly, gnawing on one pea at a time. I think she did it to torture me. But while we sat there, we did something I wasn't used to doing with a family—we talked. We conversed about our day's highs and lows, school, homework, friends, and just about anything of importance to me. They took a genuine interest in me every day. Grandma ate so slowly that dinners lasted almost an hour every evening.

Over time, I learned to treasure mealtimes. They were memorable, but more than that, they were times of simple discipleship. The table was the place where listening, planning, and training happened. At the dinner table, my grandfather spoke of simple and important things, like table manners, how to hold a conversation, and the importance of chivalry, illustrated by how he treated my grandmother. I also learned how to pray, talk about Scripture, and tackle present issues in a God-honoring way. Mealtime was the place where we convened to figure out how to take steps with God in the next twenty-four hours.

I had never experienced anything like this before. It was raw, simple, and lasting discipleship. It was the sort of training that every young man needs—and the training every godly man needs to give his sons and grandsons. It was the very best of church at the dinner table daily.

REFLECTION AND DISCUSSION QUESTIONS

1. Reflect on a man who has significantly influenced your life in good ways. What specific qualities or actions of this person have shaped your character? How can you emulate these qualities in your own journey as a man of faith?

2. How can you incorporate discipleship, as illustrated in the dinner table lessons, into your daily interactions and relationships? Consider specific areas of your life where these qualities could bring about positive change or deeper understanding.

A STORY ABOUT MAN

Most men overlook the fact that the Bible is a story spoken by God about men who were remarkably like us. It's an epic story that mirrors our own. Authored by more than forty men across millennia, this extraordinary book chronicles the saga of man. Each page, each story, is a thread in the tapestry of man's history, struggles, successes, and search for meaning. In its pages, we find reflections of ourselves, our challenges, and our most profound questions. The Bible recounts not just history but our story, inviting us to explore and connect with these timeless men and their tales.

The story unfolds with a man fashioned by God, initially pure. Yet he succumbs to the call of disobedience, tarnishing what was once pure. This pattern sets the stage for the entire Old Testament record, where this theme recurs, repeating through the lives of every man. Though diverse in abilities, qualities, and circumstances, each man stumbles down the same path of disobedience due to the inherent presence of sin.

Let's turn our gaze to the book of Genesis, where we encounter five renowned men whose lives illuminate this same pattern.

MAN ONE | NOAH

Noah was the sole obedient and righteous man in a world overrun by wickedness (Gen. 6:7–10). His willingness to obey God's command to build an enormous ark in the middle of the desert was incredible. Consider also that some people believe the earth was in a severe drought and any type of wide-reaching rainfall had never been experienced before. Whatever the case, for Noah to build the ark displayed epic faith and commitment. His faith saved his family and a remnant of earth's creatures. His start was great, but after his triumph with the ark, he showed his human imperfection, notably in an episode of drunkenness and the resultant shameful exposure (9:21).

> **The Old Testament illustrates that man, in rebellion with God, tends toward greater and more significant decline.**

MAN TWO | ABRAHAM

Abraham's life personifies faith and trust in God, especially in his willingness to obey God's command to leave his homeland and, later, to sacrifice his son Isaac. He was a man of daring faith and obedience. Yet even Abraham had moments of weakness clouded by doubt and failure, like when he misrepresented his wife, Sarah, presenting her as his sister in an effort to protect himself (Gen. 20).

MAN THREE | ISAAC

Isaac was the physical fulfillment of God's promise and the continuation of the covenant of God. However, Isaac's favoritism toward his son Esau and his deception by his son Jacob reflects a failure of discernment and leadership within his family, leading to discord and dishonesty that inflicted his family. He was a fulfillment of a promise, but he was still an imperfect man.

MAN FOUR | JACOB

Jacob's life serves as a testament to transformation and endurance. Initially resorting to deceit to gain his brother's birthright and steal his father's blessing, he sparked enduring family conflict and personal turmoil. However, his subsequent encounters with God led to a profound transformation, resulting in his being named Israel, meaning "he who strives with God."

MAN FIVE | JOSEPH

Joseph's story is one of resilience and forgiveness. Sold into slavery by his brothers, Joseph eventually rose to become an influential figure in Egypt, ultimately saving his family from famine. His ability to forgive those who had wronged him showcased immense moral strength and graciousness. Yet his youthful boasting about his dreams to his brothers revealed a lack of humility and foresight in his early years.

These are just a few of the first men in the Bible—five in all who, like every man in the story of God, had some noble qualities: righteousness, faithfulness, inheritance, perseverance, or resilience. Yet simultaneously, each man bore one or many weaknesses that exposed him, be it fallibility, deceptiveness, partiality, deceitfulness, or arrogance that led to a great fall.

This pattern persists throughout the Old Testament. It is echoed in the lives of figures like Moses, Joshua, Samuel, David, and Solomon. Each of them exhibited commendable traits alongside significant weaknesses.

The Old Testament illustrates that man, in rebellion with God, tends toward greater and more significant decline. Kingdoms are divided and destroyed. Prophets rise, calling for repentance yet often meeting resistance or neglect. Exile eventually becomes a harsh reality and a painful reminder of broken covenant and lost glory. Despite these tribulations, glimmers of hope persist in prophecies foretelling a future restoration. God's people were able to rebuild the Temple and the wall surrounding Jerusalem, but it was all in the context of a nation that had fallen from its heights.

All of these examples underscore our desperation for a man—the perfect man who could exemplify God's model of perfection.

REFLECTION AND DISCUSSION QUESTIONS

1. Reflecting on the lives of the men in the Old Testament, how do you see your own struggles mirrored in theirs? How do their moments of faith and failure connect with your own?

2. Looking back over the cycle of human imperfection in the Old Testament, would you say men are naturally geared toward seeking divine solutions? Explain why or why not.

A DIVINE MAN

While all these imperfect men had their time onstage, an underlying story was being written about another man yet to come. Scripture was systematically revealing whispers of this man through three high offices and roles: that of the prophet, priest, and king.

These three roles together form a complete picture of God's ideal man, one who embodies all three functions simultaneously. Through them, God has been instructing his people throughout history on how he communicates with humanity (seen in the role of the prophet), how he reconciles humanity (as a priest), and how he governs humanity (as a king). Each role carries significant responsibility and holds a distinct connection to God's divine plan.

In the end, only one man could fulfill each of these roles. Jesus would be the divine agent of communication, the divine plan for reconciliation, and the divine ruler of all creation.

ONE | JESUS THE DIVINE PROPHET

We begin with Jesus as the supreme prophet.

In the Old Testament, a prophet was a messenger sent to the world by God. Prophets were communicators and "seers" of things revealed by the Lord. Some were writing prophets, like Isaiah and Daniel, and others were non-writing prophets, like Elisha. Others saw visions, like Isaiah and Ezekiel, and still others lived the vision, like Hosea. There were a few who tried to stay silent, like Jeremiah, and one even tried to run from the job (Jonah). Yet all found themselves inexorably drawn back to their divine mission because they bore the burden of bringing God's message to his people and beyond.

The first of the Old Testament prophets was a man named Moses. Moses delivered a message from God that became known as the Law. Moses also led the Jewish people out of slavery in Egypt and through a forty-year desert trek culminating at the borders of Israel, the Promised Land.

As his life neared its end, Moses foretold the rise of a successor: a prophet from their ranks destined to command the people's attention. Some understood that Moses had been speaking not just of a human leader but of a supreme prophet. As time progressed, anticipation grew for this paramount prophet, who was the fulfillment of Moses's prophecy.

With undeniable clarity, the New Testament reveals that Jesus was the realization of that prophecy. During his time on earth, people recognized Jesus as, at the very least, a great prophet by the way he taught and the things he taught.

> Fear seized them all, and they glorified God, saying, "A great prophet has arisen among us!" and "God has visited his people!" (Luke 7:16)

> And the crowds said, "This is the prophet Jesus, from Nazareth of Galilee." (Matt. 21:11)

As the Prophet, Jesus flawlessly fulfilled the prophetic office.

He Was the Revelation

At the core, a prophet communicated God's Word. But Jesus was not merely a communicator of the message—he *was* the message. Jesus himself declared, "I am the way, and the truth, and the life. No one comes to the Father except through me" (John 14:6). John later testified that in Jesus, "the Word became flesh and dwelt among us, and we have seen his glory, glory as of the only Son" (John 1:14). Jesus communicated like a prophet, but he was also simultaneously the living, breathing message of God. He was unlike any man or prophet who has ever lived.

He Was the Authoritative Teacher

Prophets sent by God bore the weight of God's authority by delivering his commands and will. Jesus, as a prophet, did the same. Like Moses, he communicated new commandments, such as, "A new commandment I give to you, that you love one another" (John 13:34).

Jesus taught with unprecedented authority. Prophets of the past had declared, "God says," but Jesus frequently proclaimed, "I say to you" (Matt. 5:21–22, 27–28, 31–32, 33–34, 38–39, 43–44; John 5:24). Jesus was the ultimate Authoritative Teacher and is still unparalleled today.

He Was the Fulfillment of Prophecy

Prophets also made declarations about God's future plan. The Old Testament contains hundreds of predictive prophecies spoken over thousands of years. A significant proportion of them turned out to predict one event—the coming of the Messiah. Most theologians count over three hundred Old Testament prophecies about the Messiah. Some were fulfilled so specifically and perfectly that they are shocking to read, especially when we realize that they were written hundreds of years before Jesus lived.

Jesus was not only the prophet whom the prophets of old had predicted, but he was also the fulfillment of every prophecy that revealed him as the Messiah. He's the Prophet of prophetic prophecies.

In his role as prophet, Jesus predicted future events. He spoke of coming occurrences, like the destruction of the Temple (Matt. 24:1–2; Mark 13:1–2; Luke 21:5–6). He foretold his betrayal (Matt. 26:21–25; Mark 14:18–21; Luke 22:21–23; John 13:21–26); his suffering, death, and resurrection (Matt. 16:21; Mark 8:31–32; Luke 9:22); Peter's denial (Matt. 26:34; Mark 14:30; Luke 22:34; John 13:38); the coming of the Holy Spirit (John 14:16–17, 26; 15:26–27; 16:7–15); and more.

> Like other prophets, he foretold events, but the advent of Jesus was the main event.

Like other prophets, he foretold events, but the advent of Jesus was the main event. His life, death, and resurrection prepared all mankind for another event Jesus foretold: his second coming.

He Was the Sign and Miracle

Finally, prophets were occasionally known to perform miracles (see 1 Kings 17–18, for example). These supernatural acts validated their authority and their messages from God. But Jesus was next level. He performed countless signs and miracles that testified about God and himself. He controlled elemental matter, like when he turned water into wine, calmed storms at sea, and walked on water. He healed people of diseases and cured them of disabilities. He even raised three people from the dead, not including himself. Jesus was a prophet who performed miracles, and from beginning to end, his life was a miracle.

For centuries, God was telling us we needed a perfect prophet. Jesus is that unparalleled prophet.

And note that's just one of his three offices.

TWO | JESUS THE GREAT HIGH PRIEST

The priestly system served as the bridge between God and his people. Priests were responsible for caring for the purity of the people. They performed sacrifices, maintained the sanctity of holy sites, and imparted divine instruction. Central to their role were their duties in the Tabernacle and Temple.

The leader of the priestly order was the high priest, who had a vital role and responsibilities that set him apart. This structure foreshadowed Jesus becoming our Great High Priest.

He Was a Sinless High Priest

High priests were held to higher purity standards than any other person in Israel because they served as the nation's leading representative before God. They dressed in distinct clothing and were held to higher personal standards of ritual cleanliness. Yet no one believed that the high priest was without sin. Before performing his chief duty every year of making the sacrifices on the Day of Atonement, he sacrificed a bull to atone for his own sins and the sins of his household.

It wasn't until Jesus that we had a truly sinless high priest.

At a certain point in the Day of Atonement rituals, and for only a few moments, the high priest entered the inner sanctum of the Temple, the enclosure called the Holy of Holies, which was revered as the very presence of God on earth.

Though strict standards had been established, by the time of Jesus's birth, the entire priestly system had become compromised and corrupt.

Then came the entrance of Jesus—our Great High Priest.

The book of Hebrews intricately describes how Jesus was a superior high priest above all others. He was

> In a sense, Jesus was the Holy of Holies, the place where God and man meet.

born sinless and remained sinless. His sinless nature even granted him direct and continuous access to God's presence. In a sense, Jesus was the Holy of Holies (Heb. 9:11–12), the place where God and man meet.

Jesus is the embodiment of an eternal, superior, and permanent mediator between us and God.

He Was the Sacrifice

Finally, the high priest had one very special duty each year. On the Day of Atonement (Yom Kippur), God's people gathered in Jerusalem on the Temple grounds to seek forgiveness for their national sins. None of the other sacrifices atoned for the sin of the entire nation. This sacrifice, offered year after year, vividly reminded the people of the perpetual problem of sin and their profound need for God's atonement.

The final atonement came in the person of Jesus. Not only was he the sinless High Priest, but he was also the sacrifice itself. His sacrificial death was the last sacrifice and atonement for all sins for all time. Following his resurrection, the sacrificial system was rendered satisfied and obsolete. Jesus's life and blood encompassed the final sacrifice (1 John 2:2).

Jesus, as our final High Priest, didn't just bridge the gap between God and humanity—he eradicated it. With his sinless life, sacrificial death, and victorious resurrection, we are given an unprecedented direct line to God. We can draw near to the God who drew near to us.

And yet there is still one more role through which God revealed the story of his man.

THREE | JESUS THE SOVEREIGN KING

In the chronicles of Israel's history, there came a pivotal moment when the people of God clamored for a king. For generations, God had been their sole King. He had orchestrated victories, commissioned prophets, and established judges to shepherd his people. Still, the people of God looked jealously at neighboring kingdoms and longed to have a king.

God granted their desires, recognizing that they longed for more than a mortal ruler; they needed a King of Kings.

He Was King by Royal Appointment

Though the Jewish people had numerous corrupt and evil kings, their greatest reigning monarch was King David. The Old Testament prophesied that the Messiah would come from David's lineage (2 Sam. 7:12–16), and Jesus was indeed born from that line (Matt. 1:1–17; Luke 3:23–38).

But Jesus was also divine. He was both the son of man and the Son of God. He was conceived by God's Spirit through a virgin named Mary, who gave birth to supernatural royalty. Dignitaries from foreign lands came to pay homage to this king, whose birth was heralded in the heavens through the arrival of a new star in the night sky. In the person of Jesus, we have a King confirmed by two royal lineages: human and divine.

He Was a King Who Lived by God's Truth

Kings, as prescribed by the Mosaic Law, were to be men of God's Word (Deut. 17:18–20). Each king was to be a man governed by the Law of God. He was to write a copy of it, live by it, lead by it, learn from it, keep it, submit to it, and rule the nation by it. He was commanded to read it every day of his life. This is because man's heart, untamed by God's truth, becomes destructive—to others and to self. Every man's heart must be governed. If it is not, it will breed division with God, resulting in division with people. Because most of its kings did not abide by this, Israel had hundreds of years of slow dissolution.

Yet, in King Jesus, we have a man who both knows God's Word (Luke 2:46–49) and *is* God's Word (John 1:14). Not only did he know what was disclosed in it, he revealed what was undisclosed by becoming it in the flesh. Jesus is a King from another realm who wants us to know him and his coming kingdom.

He Was Sentenced as a King

Finally, after three years of ministry, Jesus was arrested, sentenced, and executed for being a king. Though the Jewish officials did not believe he was a king, they presented him as one to convince the Romans that Jesus was a threat to Caesar. It was the ultimate twist of God's irony in his revelation of the ultimate man.

The high priest and the Jewish religious officials understood that the Roman government would not permit them to carry out capital punishment. In Israel at that time, the sentence of death was a penalty handled only by Rome. So, the Jewish religious leaders devised a way to get the Roman governor to do their dirty work. They told Pilate that Jesus had claimed to be the "King of the Jews." Declarations like this against the Emperor of Rome were considered acts of treason punishable by death.

It was a twist of tragic irony because the title Jesus was falsely accused of claiming was, in fact, his rightful title. Jesus was, is, and always will be the King. He was sentenced and convicted as a king by his own race and religion, the spiritual leaders of Israel, even though they did not actually believe he was a king. To cap it off, Pilate posted a written notice above Jesus's head as he hung on the cross: "Jesus of Nazareth, the King of the Jews" (John 19:19).

In every language and in every time, King Jesus is rightly sentenced as the King of all Kings.

PROPHET, PRIEST, AND KING

Herein lies the ultimate point: Jesus Christ is the man.

He was the perfect Prophet, Priest, and King. He is the one creation has been longing for. In the long story of the Old Testament, God slowly and methodically prepared us so we would know one thing: that Jesus Christ is the Savior of mankind. He is the perfect representation of authentic manhood. He is God's one and only true man.

> **Herein lies the ultimate point: Jesus Christ is the man.**

Jesus is the model. He is the ideal man, the target to which all men aim. In our own way, every believing man aspires to be like him and should carry the call to reflect his glory. We are called to reflect him, our Prophet, Priest, and King. Jesus is the embodiment of perfect manhood in every way.

REFLECTION AND DISCUSSION QUESTIONS

1. Reflect on how Jesus was the ultimate Prophet, conveying God's Word in a manner distinct from the Old Testament prophets. Consider how understanding Jesus as the Word made flesh can transform your interaction with the Scriptures and the way you live out your faith daily.

2. How does Jesus, as both your High Priest and your sacrifice, alter your perspective on forgiveness and atonement? In what ways does this influence your personal communion with God and your understanding of his grace in your life?

3. How does the way Jesus exercised authority and power as King differ from worldly expectations of leadership? How can Jesus's example of kingship guide your actions, decisions, and the way you view and serve in his kingdom?

4. How has your understanding of biblical manhood been changed by understanding Jesus as the ultimate model of masculinity? How can you emulate Jesus as you interact with others in your own roles as prophet, priest, and king?

ONE MAN IN THREE STORIES

With Jesus, we encounter the epitome of divine manhood. In the grand narrative of God's unfolding story, there is only one man whose life serves as a pivotal moment for all humanity. Though Jesus appeared as one of us in human form, there was a distinctiveness about him. Examining three key events, we can gain insight into his origin, sacrifice, and salvation. Each of these momentous occasions serves as a guidepost and a path for men who desire to partake in a story that culminates in glory.

JESUS'S BIRTH (THE CHRISTMAS STORY)

The birth of Jesus is a decisive moment in God's story. It heralds the entrance of a Savior into this world. Jesus, God's Son, experienced life in human form. He is the insertion of everything man fell short of achieving.

Through the stories of every godly man in the Bible narrative, we see a dim reflection of Jesus. However, in Jesus, the reflections are resolved. We no longer see a reflection but the genuine image of the perfect man. He was born like us, yet without the stain of sin. He was a prophet who told the whole truth. He was a priest of perfection. He was a king without a character flaw.

Jesus is set apart from all other men: he is both fully God and fully man. This isn't just a theological notion but the heart of our hope and faith. He experienced everything we do—feelings, limitations, suffering—yet lived without sin. He embodies flesh while retaining the fullness of deity.

The birth of Jesus ushered into time a new story, one we affectionately call the gospel or *the good news*. That moment the angel announced to Mary that she would bear the Son of God was the moment God directly intervened in our story. Christmas is the intervention of God, the revelation of his plan to redeem men and adopt them as sons.

> **But when the fullness of time had come, God sent forth his Son, born of woman, born under the law, to redeem those who were under the law, so that we might receive adoption as sons. (Gal. 4:4–5)**

JESUS'S DEATH (THE GOOD FRIDAY STORY)

But his birth was only part one of the divine story.

Jesus grew, matured, and launched a ministry that mesmerized mankind. By divine authority and power, he performed miracles and had dominion over nature. In the gospels of Matthew, Mark, Luke, and John, we witness Jesus heal, feed, cleanse, and raise people at his command. Each event was evidence of his power over all things.

His incredible ministry came to an end in the Holy City of Jerusalem. It culminated on a Friday when Jesus was arrested, flogged, sentenced, crucified, and buried. We call it Good Friday. To passersby, it looked like nothing "good," but something was happening that was better than good. Jesus was the perfect sacrifice of the spotless Lamb of God on the Cross, willingly presented as payment for man's wages of sin that separated us from God.

This supernatural occurrence addressed the one thing man could never do: remove the sin that separated him from a relationship with God. Jesus's greatest gift to us was to address our sins by acting as the perfect high priest and as the perfect sacrifice.

> He who did not spare his own Son but gave him up for us all, how will he not also with him graciously give us all things? (Rom. 8:32)

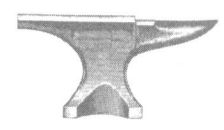

JESUS'S RESURRECTION (THE EASTER STORY)

The third part to the story is the best.

Jesus's resurrection is a momentous event. The resurrection of Christ is the ultimate victory over death. It is the centerpiece of Christianity. It's the event that alters the end of the story for every man. It changed history and all men forever. It was the moment God tore down the divine divide of sin and the barrier between man and himself. Jesus didn't just come back to life; he conquered death, never to die again. This miracle showcased his triumph over physical death and spiritual death, both of which were consequences of man's actions in the Garden. It was a display of his ultimate dominion over both realms, providing a pathway to salvation forged by God's perfect man for us all.

> Christ's resurrection is the ultimate victory over death. It is the centerpiece of Christianity. It's the event that alters the end of the story for every man.

This event isn't another chapter in man's story; it's the pinnacle moment in the story. Without Jesus's resurrection, our hope as men would be lost. But with it, everything changes, including man. It's through our belief in his death and resurrection that we can know eternal life. This belief goes beyond mere acknowledgment; it's a deep, personal faith in Jesus as the bridge between God and us, opening the door to a renewed relationship with our Creator. In him, we find the completion of God's redemptive narrative, a promise fulfilled, a hope made real for every man.

> For if while we were enemies we were reconciled to God by the death of his Son, much more, now that we are reconciled, shall we be saved by his life. (Rom. 5:10)

These three parts of Jesus's story—his birth, death, and resurrection—altered the course of history and man forever. As God's perfect man, Jesus showed us what we were called to be but could never achieve ourselves. His life is the blending of divine revelation and human perfection. Therefore, when we believe in Jesus, we are not just acknowledging a few historical events. We are surrendering to him who broke into time, defeated sin and death, and lives forevermore.

Believing in Christ's story reshapes our story. It alters our story from men wandering aimlessly and propels us into a new story filled with purpose, hope, and a renewed relationship with God. Jesus's life, death, and resurrection is the story of our redemption. It's a story that must be told and believed.

REFLECTION AND DISCUSSION QUESTIONS

1. Christmas, Good Friday, and Easter are not just celebrations and historical events but pivotal moments that transformed our relationship with God. How does this reality influence your personal faith and daily walk with God? Share a time when the power of these events and what Jesus did in them gave you hope or changed your perspective during a difficult season of your life.

2. In what ways has Jesus's story reshaped your identity? Discuss how the realization of Jesus as God's perfect man has transformed or could transform your approach to life, relationships, and faith.

STEERING OUR STORY TO HIS STORY

Back to another segment of my story.

The Saturday of my first week living in my grandparents' home proved to be quite intriguing. Grandpa left the house a bit earlier than usual, and the moment he closed the door behind him, my grandmother urged me to quickly catch up to him and join him for a ride.

I immediately abandoned what I was doing, dashed out the door, and intercepted him just as he was about to pull away. With no inkling of the destination and with minimal conversation on the way, we soon pulled up to an aging auto body shop. Following my grandfather's lead, I exited the car and followed him inside.

Upon entering the shop, I saw my grandfather's 1959 Chevy Apache truck frame resting on the floor. It took me a moment to realize what I was seeing, but soon, I noticed the truck's body suspended from the ceiling, stripped bare of paint. It was a captivating scene to behold.

My grandfather had purchased that truck brand-new in 1959, straight off the showroom floor. It had always been kept in immaculate condition and was a familiar sight in our town with its striking curves visible from blocks away. Over the years, he had repainted it in a trendy metallic gold color, popular in California during the seventies. Yet now, before me, it hung stripped of its paint, laid bare to the bone.

My grandfather entered and exchanged greetings with three body shop workers who stood in the corner conversing about his truck. They were a rugged bunch, all three with cigarettes dangling from their mouths, clearly interrupted from their smoke break by our arrival.

One of the guys extinguished his cigarette as my grandfather approached them. He nervously proclaimed, "Hey, Mr. Baker. How's it going?"

"Not bad," Grandpa responded. "How's my truck coming?"

"Well, Mr. Baker, as you can see, we've stripped off the paint. But did you know we couldn't find a single ding anywhere on the body?"

"Yep, I know that," he said. "And you better keep it that way." The other two guys laughed a little nervously. Then my grandfather made a proclamation that shocked us all.

"I want this truck done perfectly because when you are done, I plan on giving it to my grandson here when he turns sixteen."

The shop guys, of course, looked appalled at the notion of eventually turning over this beauty to a teenager. But you have to know, I was utterly surprised as well. I had been at his house barely a week, and now he planned to give me his prized possession.

As we drove away, my grandfather reiterated his offer, but with a single condition: "You're going to have to learn how to drive Liz." That was the truck's name—Elizabeth, or Liz for short. My grandfather often joked that it was his only love affair with another woman.

A couple of months later, my grandfather drove home with a fully restored truck. Gleaming in fire-engine red, it was polished to perfection. The front end shined with chrome accents, while the bed showcased oak slats, and the interior was adorned with luxurious leather. Essentially, it was a show truck that my grandfather used daily to run errands to the golf course and hardware store. It was a well-known sight around town. But learning to drive it was a riveting experience.

In the following months, my grandfather coached me from the passenger seat as I learned the ins and outs of driving this classic car. I soon discovered that this truck didn't have a single automatic feature. With its bus-like steering wheel and lack of power steering, maneuvering from a standstill was a colossal task. The three-on-the-tree non-synchronized transmission posed its own challenges; shifting into first gear required a complete stop, lest I incur a backhand from Grandpa.

Liz featured a starter located on the floor, requiring me to nearly slide out of my seat to reach it, as the seats were not adjustable. Seat belts were nonexistent in this truck. The windows were manually lowered using a crank, and we affectionately referred to the wing windows as the "air conditioner," given the truck's lack of one. Driving Liz was an adventure unlike any other.

Then, my day finally came. I passed my written test, earning my driver's permit. The very next request to my grandfather was, "Can we take Liz for a drive?" Without hesitation, he agreed.

Only a few months after her complete restoration, I found myself in the driver's seat of the most recognizable truck in town, armed with a driver's permit barely two hours old. I ignited the engine and smoothly shifted her into first gear. We took off down the street effortlessly. Those first five blocks were the highlight of my life. I bounced around on the spring-loaded seat, sporting a wide grin that stretched from ear to ear. Until I encountered my first stop.

It was a stop sign situated atop a steep hill, a feature of the area I had never paid much attention to before. But it wasn't just a slight incline; it was a timeless California hill—steep and intimidating. All my elation from the previous five blocks evaporated instantly.

Under Grandpa's watchful eyes, I executed precisely what he had taught me. I firmly pressed down on the brake and clutch pedals. With my right hand, I moved the shifter into first gear. Then, transitioning my right hand from the shifter to the steering wheel, I prepared to navigate the daunting ascent.

However, by this point, a car had pulled up behind me—an old brown beater of some sort. I felt a surge of nervousness as the vehicle pulled up uncomfortably close to the truck's rear bumper. I'm not sure why the driver pulled up so close.

Recalling the training of my grandfather for the occasional hill stop, I reached for the emergency brake with my left hand. If I timed my actions just right, engaging the brake might halt the rollback long enough for me to engage the clutch, release the brake, and press the gas pedal. With my foot moving from the brake to the gas, I began the tricky process of working the clutch. In essence, I was employing every limb in my body to maneuver that truck.

As soon as my grandfather saw me reach for the emergency brake, he realized what was happening. He adjusted his bifocals and looked in the passenger-side mirror, noticing that the sedan was way too close. I could feel him staring me down, but I had way too much going on to make eye contact with him. "Son," he said, crossing his arms, "you better not scratch my truck!"

His serious and declarative tone put the fear of God in me. The only thing I knew to do was give it more gas to prevent the truck from drifting rearward. So I revved up the engine of that inline-six, taking it from a steady 2,000 rpms up to a humming 4,000 rpms. My plan was to mash on the gas and release that clutch. I knew it might not be smooth, but I refused to roll back and scratch my grandfather's prized possession.

Recognizing my intentions, Grandpa promptly intervened, ordering me to stop. He directed me to stop and shift the truck back into neutral. I suppose he assumed that the other car would either wait or drive around us.

Then we both sat there for a few seconds in silence trying to get a handle on this very tense moment.

Finally, he broke the silence and tension with a question, "Did I make you nervous?"

I nodded slowly.

"Can I give you some advice?"

I nodded in agreement, and then he gave me the most ridiculous advice.

"When I was a kid, and I was learning to drive, just like you, on my father's Model T. In situations like this hill, we used to just let the car roll backward and gently rest the car on the bumper of the car behind us. And then we'd take off."

That was his advice? I thought he had lost his mind. I was certain there was no chance that the freshly dipped and polished chrome bumper on the rear of this truck would align with the bumper of the car behind me. I stared at him in disbelief, and then he continued.

"But whatever you do, make sure you don't put a scratch on my truck!"

This advice was more laughable than advisable. Yet, while we were conversing, the car behind us rolled back to give me enough room to proceed. Seizing the opportunity, I quickly dropped the truck into first gear, released the clutch, and gave that truck just enough gas that it sputtered and skipped over the hill with minimum rollback.

It might seem strange to hear this, but that scene was undeniably one of the most profound moments of my teen years. It marked the first time in my life that I had a man by my side in a challenge of life. Unlike my father and stepfather, who were rarely present, my grandfather cherished being with me. He was personally invested in my success, eager to pour into me, and even entrusted me with his most treasured possession. But I would soon learn that this truck and the relationship that was forged with my grandpa were merely a means of introducing me to another man—Jesus.

ONE MAN WHO POINTED TO ANOTHER

Over the following three months, Grandpa faithfully trained me in the art of handling Liz. Every Saturday morning was dedicated to hours spent honing my skills in that old truck—starting with the basics of parallel parking. In the first month, we focused on mastering parking in flat areas. The following month, we tackled inclining hills, and in the third month, we sharpened my skills on those declining slopes.

Parallel parking in that truck was challenging. It didn't have all the automatic features of trucks today. We would navigate the streets of the Bay Area, and my grandfather would point to spots where he wanted me to park.

Each time we parked, he insisted that I switch off the truck, creating an opportunity for a conversation. My grandfather recognized that he had me trapped in a setting where he could actively disciple me. In that truck, our discussions spanned all kinds of topics—women, men, life, careers, talents, manners, challenges, and problems. But above all else, they somehow diverted to a man named Jesus.

On one of those occasions when we were parked by the roadside, he initiated one of the most profound conversations we ever had. It unfolded like this:

"Son, I know your mom and dad say that God is not real because Christians are hypocrites and the church is full of broken people." He paused and locked eyes with me to ensure I was listening. "And you should know, they're right. Christians are hypocrites, and the church is full of broken people. In fact, I can act like a hypocrite because I am a broken person. But you need to know I don't put my faith in hypocrites or broken people but in a man who did what he said he would do and whose body was broken for you and me. That man was Jesus Christ."

That brief thirty-second exchange completely shifted my perspective on everything about Jesus. Grandpa made it a habit to engage in these short conversations at every stop. While short, they were profound. Week after week for those three months, those conversations staked up and had a profound impact on my life.

As I look back on those formative months spent with my grandfather driving Liz, it's clear to me now that our time together wasn't just about learning to drive a vintage truck around the streets of our town. It was about something much more significant.

Given his patient coaching and intentional conversations, my grandfather was not just imparting driving skills; he was sharing wisdom about life, relationships, and faith. And woven through it all was the recurring theme of a man named Jesus.

My grandfather understood something profound: True manhood isn't just about physical strength, monetary success, or career accomplishment. It's about following Jesus Christ's ultimate example of manhood, about surrendering to the one who is the man—our prophet, priest, and king.

Through his words and actions, my grandfather showed me that Jesus isn't just another man like Noah, Abraham, Isaac, Jacob, or Joseph. He's the epitome of true manhood, perfect in all his ways. The only man worth emulating.

> **It takes a man to tell a man the true story about a man so he can become a man.**

In the same way, I hope this book is for you like those drives were for me. I implore you to consider Jesus's example. Let him be your guide, role model, source of strength, and Lord. Then let his life and teachings shape your own journey toward authentic manhood. Because, in the end, it's not about the trucks we own or the accomplishments we achieve. It's about the men we are. There's no better model to follow than the one who gave everything for us—Jesus Christ, the ultimate man.

As my grandfather used to say: it takes a man to tell a man the true story about a man so he can become a man.

REFLECTION AND DISCUSSION QUESTIONS

1. Think about someone who has actively or passively mentored you. How did this person guide you toward understanding and embodying true manhood

and faith? Reflect on specific moments or lessons that significantly shaped your journey.

2. Reflect on the impact that Vince's grandfather had on him. How can you use your own life stories and experiences to effectively communicate and impart the truth about Jesus, mankind, and faith to other men, including young men you know and have influence over?

THE REPENTANT MAN

MY TURN

During my twenties, I was adrift, like many other guys at this stage of life. My family ties were tenuous, and my social ties were with all the wrong people. Despite attempts at college, I struggled to find my calling and dropped out twice. My current job didn't leverage my strengths, and I sought fulfillment in empty endeavors, which left me feeling hollow inside. It was a challenging period, but it served as the catalyst for a profound transformation in my life.

I eventually embraced the fact that all my present circumstances were the result of my foolish choices. The anguish during this time was indescribable—I finally had hit rock bottom. There I was, alone and directionless, facing one of the darkest chapters of my life.

But I am getting too far ahead in the story. Let's jump back five years.

As I've already noted, when I was fifteen, I moved in with my grandparents. On Sunday mornings, sleeping in was not an option. Attending church was nonnegotiable as long as I lived with Grandpa. That was simply the way it was—no room for debate.

My grandfather was one of the founding members of this small church. It was the type where a "busy" day meant around thirty attendees, most of whom were elderly. Frankly, it was a challenging experience. The singing was hit-or-miss, the prayers seemed to stretch on endlessly, and the teaching, led by various individuals, often left me confused. The most frustrating part? I had no idea when those seemingly endless services would finally conclude.

But it was in this tiny church during one of those Sunday sermons that I perked up.

Sitting there on a stiff, cold, uncomfortable pew, feeling alone and forgotten, I heard the preacher say something that caught my attention. "If you read Colossians 3 every day for a month," he said, "it will change your life forever." I can't recall the totality of the message, but that line resounded in my mind, "I promise it will change your life forever."

Motivated by curiosity and hopeful that God would fulfill his promise, I borrowed an old Bible from my grandparents. I brought it down to my room and diligently read Colossians 3 every single day for thirty consecutive days. Some days, I read it once; on others, multiple times. I was putting God to the test, eager to see if he would indeed come through as the preacher had claimed. I firmly believed that at the end of this thirty-day challenge, God was going to reveal himself in some profound way to me, transforming my life, circumstances, and feelings of loneliness forever.

Each of the thirty days, my anticipation grew. Finally, on the thirtieth day, I opened the Bible, read Colossians 3 one last time, closed the Good Book … and then waited. I sat for a moment or two, and guess what happened?

Nothing. That's right, nothing.

That experience had the opposite effect on me; it turned out to be a significant disappointment. Actually, I felt embarrassed by how much hope I had placed in the preacher's promise. Instead of drawing me closer to God, it drove me further away from him. In the subsequent months, I gradually drifted from God, doubting his willingness to intervene in my life. However, one unintended outcome emerged from those thirty days: I had unintentionally memorized the entirety of Colossians 3.

Now, let's pick back up where I started this story.

After a night of partying with some acquaintances whose names and faces now escape me, I woke up alone in a random apartment. A wave of loneliness and despair engulfed me as I struggled to make sense of my surroundings. Dragging myself out of bed, I stumbled toward a mirror mounted above a grimy sink on the wall. Staring back at me was a distorted reflection as if I were peering into a fun-house mirror. My vision was still clouded by the remnants of substances from the previous night, and despite rubbing my eyes, clarity evaded me.

Overwhelmed by my foolishness, a deep emptiness and sadness came over me as I reflected on the drift of my life over the last many months. Profoundly unsettled, I began to talk out loud to the only person available—God. I asked him a single question as I stared at my reflection in the mirror: "God, is this all there is? I am ready to listen if you will speak. Just let me know what to do."

Suddenly, it was like God transported me back years in time. I was sitting in that old church again, on that same unforgiving pew, listening to that preacher proclaim, "If you read Colossians 3 every day for a month, it will change your life forever." The promise, which I hadn't thought about in a few years, flooded back into my mind. As I peered into the mirror, every word came flooding back from Colossians 3. I found myself reciting the verses out loud as I stared at the reflection of that lost young man in the mirror.

> If then you have been raised with Christ, seek the things that are above, where Christ is, seated at the right hand of God. Set your minds on things that are above, not on things that are on earth. For you have died, and your life is hidden with Christ in God. When Christ who is your life appears, then you also will appear with him in glory. (Col. 3:1-4)

From the opening verse to the final word, I recited every line of that chapter. It felt as though a divine voice resonated from the heavens, passing through Paul's pen to the congregation at Colossae, then through the preacher, and finally reaching me. In that moment, it was as if God himself spoke directly to the lost soul gazing back at me in the mirror. It was his message, his spoken word, tailored specifically for me.

As I stood there, face to face with my own brokenness and desperation, God's word from Colossians 3 resounded in my mind with newfound clarity. It was as if every word, every verse, was speaking directly to the farthest reaches of my soul, piercing through the haze of my confusion and despair.

> "God, is this all there is? I am ready to listen if you will speak. Just let me know what to do."

In those moments of thoughtful introspection, I realized the extent of my folly and the consequences of my rebellious choices. The emptiness I felt was not just the absence of purpose or direction; it was the weight of my sin, bearing down on me like an anchor dragging me into the depths.

But God, in his infinite mercy and grace, used that moment of brokenness to convict me of my need for repentance and transformation. Through his word, he revealed the truth about my condition—that I was lost but not beyond his reach, broken but not beyond his healing.

As I recited the verses of Colossians 3, each word became a beacon of hope, illuminating the path toward redemption and restoration. It was a divine invitation to turn away from my wayward ways and fix my gaze on the things above, where Christ rules and reigns supreme.

And so, in that dingy apartment, surrounded by the remnants of my recklessness, I made a choice—a choice to heed God's call, to surrender my life again to his will, and to follow Jesus wholeheartedly.

From that moment on, my life took on new meaning and purpose. The despair that once engulfed me was replaced by a sense of peace and assurance—a peace that transcends understanding and an assurance that comes from knowing I am loved and forgiven by the One who gave his life for me.

Looking back, I realize that God's word truly did change my life forever. It convicted me of my sin, drove me toward repentance, and set me on a path of transformation and renewal. Though the journey has been challenging at times, I am grateful for every step, knowing that God is with me for every one of those steps along the way.

Back then, I was unsure of how to take that next step forward. But deep down, I knew it was imperative to do so immediately, or risk never taking the step at all.

REFLECTION AND DISCUSSION QUESTIONS

1. Have you experienced a rock-bottom moment like the one described, where you felt lost and without direction? How did this moment serve as a transition for you in pursuing a relationship with God or toward making some serious changes in your life?

2. Can you think of a time when a particular scripture or biblical teaching unexpectedly resonated with you and influenced a change in your perspective or life direction? How did this experience deepen your understanding of God's presence and guidance in your life?

THE HEART OF CHANGE

At that moment, I was experiencing the initial stirrings of repentance. Repentance holds a central place in God's Word, serving as the cornerstone of the gospel message and the catalyst for genuine transformation in a man's life. It was so central and essential that it's no coincidence that both John and Jesus began their ministries preaching the vital message of repentance.

Here's how John proclaimed it:

> In those days John the Baptist came preaching in the wilderness of Judea, "Repent, for the kingdom of heaven is at hand." (Matt. 3:1-2)

Then, shortly after, here's how Jesus echoed it:

> From that time Jesus began to preach, saying, "Repent, for the kingdom of heaven is at hand." (Matt. 4:17)

These divinely appointed men weren't mincing words. They were preaching the message that all men need to hear: "Repent!"

But what exactly does that word mean?

This term is pervasive throughout both the Old and New Testaments, emphasizing two fundamental concepts reiterated consistently.

CONCEPT ONE | GODLY REGRET

First, repentance encompasses a profound regret that strikes when one recognizes disobedience to God's commands and the abandonment of his authority. Recall our earlier discussion on sin in chapter 2. Repentance isn't merely remorse over being caught; it's about sincerely regretting the sin itself and acknowledging accountability for one's actions. It involves grasping the seriousness and far-reaching consequences of one's sin.

CONCEPT TWO | GODLY CHANGE

Second, repentance demands obedient action. It's not confined to a fleeting emotion but leads to transformed behavior. It's not merely adjusting one aspect of behavior; it's a holistic reversal, turning away from disobedience and aligning your heart, mind, and actions with God's commands. It represents a comprehensive change in your approach to life.

Many believers get tripped up over this because *repentance* isn't a word we hear often. But understanding what it means is crucial if we are going to take steps toward it. Repentance is not merely feeling sorry for a mistake; it's feeling regret for rejecting God's authority (2 Cor. 7:10). It's not to be confused with confession, even though it involves confessing our sin and rebellion to God (Rom. 10:9). Repentance does not save us, but it does express the belief that Jesus saves us (Acts 11:18).

Repentance demands both godly regret and godly change. However, it poses challenges for men beyond simply understanding the term. It requires profound introspection and a fundamental shift in our worldview. Repentance calls for humility to acknowledge our faults and the courage to admit when we're wrong. It requires surrender and a readiness to adjust our ways to align with God's. None of these tasks are easy for men. Yet if we confront these challenges, we can navigate through the process and begin taking steps of genuine repentance.

REFLECTION AND DISCUSSION QUESTIONS

1. In what areas of your life do you sense the need for godly regret or godly change? Reflect on how acknowledging these can lead you toward a deeper, more authentic relationship with God.

2. Think about a time when you experienced true repentance. How did it differ from simply feeling sorry for your actions? Reflect on how this experience deepened your understanding of forgiveness, grace, and salvation.

THE STEPS OF GENUINE REPENTANCE

It often helps to see how conceptual and theological concepts like repentance play out in real-life stories to understand them. So, let's do that. Let's examine repentance through the Parable of the Prodigal Son, a story we have already referenced.

In this parable, Jesus paints an incredible portrait of the journey of genuine repentance, offering a tangible example of what it entails.

> But when he came to himself, he said, "How many of my father's hired servants have more than enough bread, but I perish here with hunger! I will arise and go to my father, and I will say to him, 'Father, I have sinned against heaven and before you. I am no longer worthy to be called your son. Treat me as one of your hired servants.'" And he arose and came to his father. But while he was still a long way off, his father saw him and felt compassion, and ran and embraced him and kissed him. And the son said to him, "Father, I have sinned against heaven and before you. I am no longer worthy to be called your son." (Luke 15:17–21)

This teaching contains an incredibly remarkable description of four steps of genuine repentance that reshape and remake men.

STEP ONE | AWARENESS

But when he came to himself … (Luke 15:17)

The initial phase of repentance involves becoming aware of your situation. It's about waking up to the reality of your actions and recognizing the need for change.

This awakening moment was pivotal for the Prodigal Son. Suddenly, everything clicked. He saw his decisions, motivations, and their consequences with startling clarity. He could now compare the outcomes of his chosen path with the life his father offered. This epiphany marked a crucial turning point and a profound moment of clarity.

But this is only where repentance begins.

STEP TWO | REGRET

Father, I have sinned against heaven and before you.
(Luke 15:18, 21)

The next step in the process involves expressing godly regret for turning away from God's authority and commands. It's about feeling genuine remorse for your sins and the implications of these sins.

His confession reflects his remorse. His godly regret leads to immediate acknowledgment, which he verbalizes by confessing his sin against both God and man. Notice the sequence of his regretful confession: heaven first and man second. Jesus used this intentional order to bring attention to genuine godly regret.

In this step, the Prodigal Son takes ownership. He doesn't make excuses or shift blame; instead, he recognizes the gravity of his wrongdoing and its impact on his relationship with God and others. By uttering the words "I have sinned," the son demonstrates his genuine remorse and regret for the offense he has committed, which is an essential aspect of true repentance.

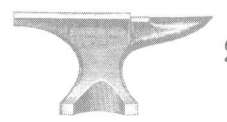

STEP THREE | ACTION

I will arise and go. (Luke 15:18)

In this third step of genuine repentance, the Prodigal Son moves beyond mere awareness and regret to decisive action. He doesn't remain inactive, ruminating on his remorse, but actively takes steps to reconcile his regrets with his father.

By declaring, "I will arise and go," the son verbalizes his commitment. His words are not empty promises but a resolve to physically return to his father and request forgiveness. This is essential in genuine repentance. Godly action signifies a turn from sin and a willingness to reconcile with God and others.

It's vital for men to understand that true repentance requires more than feelings of remorse; it necessitates tangible action. Merely feeling sorry for doing something wrong is not enough. We must close the gap between feelings of conviction and actions of conviction by stepping from disobedience to obedience to show we are repentant.

> **We must close the gap between feelings of conviction and actions of conviction by stepping from disobedience to obedience to show we are repentant.**

STEP FOUR | SURRENDER

> **I am no longer worthy to be called your son. Treat me as one of your hired servants. (Luke 15:19, 21)**

In this final stage of genuine repentance, the Prodigal exhibits complete surrender to his father. He doesn't just seek forgiveness for his actions but relinquishes his entire identity and way of life.

The son's humility and contrition are evident as he expresses his desire to serve his father as a nameless slave. He acknowledges his unworthiness of sonship and offers himself humbly to his father.

This step underscores the profound transformation that occurs through repentance. It's not merely about seeking forgiveness for past wrongs but about surrendering one's will and identity to God completely. True repentance involves a radical shift in perspective from self-centeredness to God-centeredness and a willingness to submit to his authority and guidance.

If I were to rewrite what the Prodigal said in my own words, it would read: "Father, I left rejecting you and your ways. I wanted to live my own way, and I wanted my own identity. I see now how wrong I was and how I've wronged you. I am undeserving of sonship. Would you have room in your heart and home to let me serve you as a nameless slave? I will serve you quietly in the fields alongside the other servants. I only want to live under your care, protection, and provision."

This is the heartfelt admission of a son who has completely embraced surrender. He has recognized his need for a Savior to rescue him and a Lord to guide him.

But as we read this story, it's crucial to remember that this wasn't a surrender to any ordinary man. In this parable, the father symbolizes God, the Father of all humanity. Therefore, this story and the scene beautifully illustrate authentic repentance, characterized by awareness, remorse, decisive steps, and submission.

But to clarify repentance even further, let's consider what repentance is not.

REPENTANCE IS NOT

At times, grasping an abstract yet significant theological concept like repentance requires understanding what it isn't. To illustrate incomplete repentance, all we must do is continue reading the parable. Jesus didn't merely illustrate what true repentance looks like; he also gave us a clear indication of what falls short.

Later in the story, he went on to explain:

> But [the older son] was angry and refused to go in. His father came out and entreated him, but he answered his father, "Look, these many years I have served you, and I never disobeyed your command, yet you never gave me a young goat, that I might celebrate with my friends. But when this son of yours came, who has devoured your property with prostitutes, you killed the fattened calf for him!" And he said to him, "Son, you are always with me, and all that is mine is yours. It was fitting to celebrate and be glad, for this your brother was dead, and is alive; he was lost, and is found." (Luke 15:28–32)

The older son's true nature was exposed by his own words. Notice his absence of awareness, remorse, action, or surrender. The glaring disparity between the two brothers is evident. Jesus juxtaposed two archetypes: the self-absorbed younger son who embodied genuine repentance and the self-righteous older son who remained oblivious, unrepentant, resistant, and unyielding. This prompts us to ponder if the older son will remain outside the home or potentially reconcile with the father.

As we reflect on the Parable of the Prodigal Son, we're confronted not just with the older son's fate but also with our own fate. Do we resemble the older son, consumed by self-righteousness and blind to our need for reconciliation? Or do we resemble the younger son, humbly recognizing our faults and seeking forgiveness?

The choice is ours to make.

Just as the father eagerly awaited the return of his wayward son, our heavenly Father eagerly awaits our return. But we must take the necessary steps to find our way back. We must acknowledge our faults, repent of our sins, and surrender to the loving embrace of our Father.

So, will you turn from your self-centeredness and self-righteousness and embrace the grace and forgiveness that await you?

The choice is yours. But I implore you, come home to the Father. He is waiting for you with open arms.

REFLECTION AND DISCUSSION QUESTIONS

1. When have you experienced a coming-to-yourself moment like the Prodigal Son did? How did this moment lead you to a place of godly regret and a realization of your actions against God and others? Share a time when this awareness led you to take responsibility for your actions rather than blame others or make excuses.

2. Reflect on a time when you felt convicted of wrongdoing. Did you take immediate action to correct your path, or did you linger in a state of remorse without change? Share the challenges and the importance of moving from feeling convicted to taking decisive action. Additionally, contemplate all the steps of complete surrender as depicted by the Prodigal Son. How can this principle of surrender be applied in your own life, especially in the context of your relationship with God and others?

THE LONG WAY HOME

Back to my story.

My journey of repentance began with a hard and long first step. Following that awakening in Colossians 3, prompted by God, the only destination I felt drawn to was home: my grandparents' home.

At the time, I drove an old 1959 VW truck (not the '59 Chevy Apache I'd learned to drive in). It was packed with horsepower from an air-cooled 36-horsepower engine. There were two problems: First, my grandparents' home was about 140 miles from where I was currently living. Second, my truck's manual transmission was stuck in second gear. If I were going to head home, it would mean enduring a grueling, humiliating twenty-mile-per-hour drive for about seven hours. But I had no choice. I packed up my belongings and headed home.

The drive was painful in every way—physically, emotionally, and spiritually. That truck beat me down.

Just imagine me leaning over that steering wheel for seven hours. All thirty-six of those horses screamed in the back, topping out at a whopping twenty miles per hour. As the engine got hot, black smoke billowed out the back. I had to turn the heater on just to vent the heat off that old air-cooled engine. Then the cab filled with hot air, so I rolled the windows down, flipped the wing windows open, and propped up the front safari windows. The air was blowing at me from every direction as cars flew past, observing the spectacle.

During those hours, I had a lot of time to think. I reflected on my decisions, mistakes, and current issues. My mind was stirred by what my grandparents would think when I pulled up to their home. In the previous months, I had burned some bridges with them, and my imagination invented many mental images about how they might respond. My sin and shame and the consequences of my past actions played over and over in my mind.

And then, about halfway home, I turned on my old transistor radio. I could barely hear it, with the engine blaring and the air blowing. But right when I turned it on, a song by an old poet named Bob Dylan came across the airwave. The song: "Like a Rolling Stone." It's all about disillusionment, loss of status, and feeling adrift in the world.

As I sang along, the words had an interesting spiritual effect: I burst into tears.

Try to imagine what this looked like. A young man crying as he puttered down the freeway at twenty miles per hour, smoke barreling out the back, engine screaming, windows open, and Bob Dylan cranked on the radio. I'm sure I was quite the sight for passersby. But honestly, I didn't care. There was one thing on my mind—getting home.

Then, after seven brutal hours, I arrived.

I hit the brakes, and the truck all but died. I just laid my arms and head on that steering wheel, knowing I was about to make the most challenging walk of my life. But I had no choice. That truck was smoked. I had to get out.

I peeled my sweaty legs from the seat, stretched my back, and walked up to the front of my grandparents' small, humble home. I could see through their large floor-to-ceiling window. There sat the two recliners where my grandparents relaxed during the day. Both chairs faced the television with their backs to the window. My grandmother was absent, probably in the kitchen, but Grandpa was reclining in his. I saw him leaning back with his arms stretched out behind his shiny bald head. I suddenly felt so torn about the monumental task of walking up the stairway to the door. I was halted by my unholiness, considering my grandfather's generosity, love, and faithfulness to both God and me.

I lowered my head and continued to take one hard step after another. As I neared the stairway at the front of the house, I noticed that my grandfather had vacated his chair. For a split second, the thought of escape crossed my mind. Then the front door opened.

Grandpa looked down at me from the top step. Before I could utter a word, he turned toward the kitchen and shouted, "Grandma, our son has come home." (Notice his words. I did not realize it at the time, but he was calling me a prodigal son.)

Without reservation, my grandfather spread his arms and embraced me with a long, warm hug. This was not the welcome I had expected. It wasn't anything like what I'd seen in my imagination. This moment and the conversation that followed marked a significant turn in my spiritual life. My grandparents made it clear that I was welcomed home, on the condition that I make some changes that I was completely willing to make.

This is the hard road of repentance. At least, this is what the first few steps in my life looked like. There was awareness of sin, godly regret, obedient action, and ongoing surrender to the Lord. And then I just took one step after another of daily repentance.

In the months that followed, I experienced a radical transformation. The burdens of guilt and shame were replaced with a newfound sense of purpose and joy. Each day became an opportunity to walk in obedience, knowing that I was loved beyond measure.

Looking back on that pivotal moment, I'm reminded that repentance isn't about dwelling on past mistakes; it's about stepping into the abundant life that God has promised. It's about letting go of the baggage of sin and embracing the freedom that comes from his forgiveness.

My journey of repentance continues, but I walk it with confidence, knowing that I am not alone. God's grace is sufficient, his love is unending, and his mercy is new every morning. And as I continue to walk in repentance, I am perpetually amazed by the beauty of God's redeeming love.

How about you? Are you taking steps of daily repentance? Or perhaps you've never experienced this before. Well, guess what? You can start right now. You can come home to the Father, just as I did.

If you're ready to take that first step, here's a simple prayer you can pray to mark the first step of man in your journey toward a life of repentance:

> *Father,*
>
> *I come to you just as I am, with all my faults and failures. I recognize that I've strayed from your path, and I'm sorry. Please forgive me for my sins. I choose to turn away from my old life and follow you wholeheartedly. Thank you for your love and grace that welcome me home. Help me to walk in repentance every day, surrendering to your will and experiencing the freedom and joy that come from your forgiveness.*
>
> *In Jesus's name, amen.*

Let the Father embrace you with his love and grace. Your journey of repentance starts now, and he will walk with you every step of the way.

Welcome home, brother. Repentance is the red-hot forge where God's men are made.

REFLECTION AND DISCUSSION QUESTIONS

1. Did you pray the prayer above? If so, tell a Christian believer in your life that today is the day you repented of your sins. Encourage them to pray for you and invite them to help you take the next few steps in your spiritual life.

2. Like Vince's long and challenging drive in the story, have you ever experienced a "long return" in your spiritual life that felt arduous and exposed you? Share how this return, with its hardships, helped you realize the ongoing need for repentance in your walk with God.

3. How does Vince's return home resonate with your own experiences of repentance and surrender to God? Discuss a time you took steps toward repentance and reconciliation with God and others in your life. How are you a different man today because of these occurrences?

THE MAN WHO LISTENS

"Honey, did you hear me?" my wife recently asked.

"Of course I did," I declared with confidence. Yet in my head, a little voice whispered, *Now, what did she say?*

This is how most men listen. They are tuned out to one voice because they are so attuned to another. And they are so ashamed to admit that they weren't listening, they would rather lie about listening than confess the truth.

> **If we don't learn how to listen to Jesus, it will block our progress and growth as men.**

Superficial listening is a challenge in any relationship. I am guilty of it too. But in our spiritual lives, if we don't start listening, we will find ourselves in all the trouble we presented in the first four chapters of this book. If we don't learn how to listen to Jesus, it will block our progress and growth as men.

So that is where we are headed: learning how to listen as a man to the Man.

THE FOUR VOICES ALL MEN HEAR

Most men have trouble listening to God, which results in grave consequences in their lives.

Returning to that familiar Genesis story, we'll discover that the origin of sin was brought on because man didn't listen to God. He was given a divine command directly by God, and this before woman was created. It was his responsibility to hear, communicate, and steward obedience to God's command. It was his failure to do this that ushered in sin and all its effects. His unwillingness to hear and heed God's voice transformed trusting obedience into willful disobedience. It was all brought on because he failed to listen to God, choosing instead to listen to the other voices stirring around in his head.

Men won't admit this, but we have "voices" stirring around in our heads. These internal voices are powerfully persuasive yet tragically misleading. As men dedicated to God, we need to know and identify the whisper of these deceptive voices—because they can deter us from obedience to God's voice, which requires awareness, discernment, and action.

Therefore, as God's men, we must master the art of both rejecting the wrong voices and embracing the right one. Often, our egos clamor loudly, drowning out the gentle whispers of God. Many men, including myself in the example with my wife, tend to listen superficially, carrying this same tendency into our relationship with God. This dual task requires active engagement; it's not a passive endeavor but demands consistent effort and practice. Developing the ability to listen to God is a pivotal aspect of our faith journey. It enables us to align more closely with his will, granting us the strength and confidence to live out our faith authentically and boldly. With that, let's unpack four voices.

In my years of ministering to men, I've identified four voices that are most often stirring in their minds. The first three are deceptive and lead men astray. The last one is wonderfully revealing, offers profound insights and direction, and results in incredible outcomes in a godly man's life.

ONE | THE VOICE OF PRIDE

The first is obvious. It's the voice of pride. This should surprise no one since pride is a common call in the minds of men. It's a seductive and misleading voice. I call this "the voice of the man you think you are." Its whisper has a powerful influence on a man's life. What makes it so alluring is that its call is distinct to each man. The voice of pride is uniquely attuned to our personal weaknesses and selfish desires, making it a master of deception.

Let me illustrate.

Below are eight distinct manifestations of pride, each with its own unique workings and inner voice that tempts and persuades a man. These manifestations highlight the various ways pride infiltrates our thoughts and actions, subtly enticing men into an arrogant fall.

> **Unwillingness**—Sometimes a man may perceive pride as a voice that brushes off new ideas or suggestions. This voice persuades him that his own way is the sole correct path, resulting in a rigid and inflexible stance. He might internally rationalize, *Why change what's already working for me?*
>
> **Judgmentalism**—In this form, pride whispers criticisms of others, often unjustified, to make the man feel superior. He might find himself constantly evaluating others, thinking, *I would never make that mistake* or *I'm better than them because …*
>
> **Control**—Here, pride manifests as a voice urging the man to take charge, even in situations where it's not his place. It feeds on the drive for power and influence, saying, *If I don't control this, it will go wrong* or *Only I know how to handle this.*
>
> **Self-Reliance**—Pride in this form inflates a man's confidence in his abilities to an unrealistic level. He hears a voice saying, *I don't need anyone's help* or *Asking for help is a sign of weakness.*

> **Defensiveness**—This aspect of pride acts as a shield against criticism or advice. The voice of pride might say, *They're just trying to bring me down* or *I don't need to listen to this; I know I'm right.*
>
> **Comparative Mindset**—Pride often fuels a comparative mindset, where the man constantly measures himself against others, leading to feelings of superiority or envy. Thoughts like *I'm more successful than them* or *Why do they have what I don't?* are common.
>
> **Accountability Avoidant**—When pride leads to shirking ownership or denying mistakes, it often sounds like *That wasn't my fault* or *They're just trying to blame me for their mistakes.*
>
> **Spiritual Complacency**—In this state, pride convinces a man that he doesn't need spiritual growth or deeper connections. He might think, *I'm doing fine on my own* or *I don't need to change anything about my spiritual life.*

In each of these examples, the whisper of pride is subtle and powerful. If given too much time and credence, these voices will mature into self-justifying thoughts that lead a man to do things that are far from righteous.

> **Every man knows another man whose pride has gone to his head. It was in his head; it inflated his head until, finally, it came to a head.**

But here's what makes pride insidious: it tailors its voice uniquely to you. This means you must know the unique call of the voice of pride that persuades you. Only you can identify the voice and recognize the persuasion when it speaks.

You must get a handle on this sooner rather than later because pride is destructive. Every man knows another man whose pride has gone to his head. It was in his head; it inflated his head until, finally, it came to a head. We all know at least one man who has let this voice coerce him until it controlled him. Sometimes, we are that man. And as Proverbs 16:18 states, "Pride goes before destruction, and a haughty spirit before a fall."

REFLECTION AND DISCUSSION QUESTIONS

1. Which of these eight manifestations of the voice of pride resonates most with you? How has it influenced your thoughts and actions?

2. Reflect on moments when the voice of pride may have led you away from the call of God. What does your unique voice of pride sound like? What prideful actions result from hearing it? How can you attune to the voice of God when this occurs?

TWO | THE VOICE OF THE PLEASER

Another voice that relentlessly echoes in the minds of men is the one that compels them to please others. It's the voice of "the man that others expect him to be." This man is mistakenly guided by the wonderful plans others have for his life.

The voice of the pleaser lures men in with the promise of acceptance and success. It persuades men that fulfillment will come from aligning with what others—bosses, coaches, teachers, friends, or family—expect and desire from them. Thus, men reshape their lives, character, values, beliefs, and actions to suit the admiration of others. But this only results in a life drained by the overwhelming array of others' opinions.

People-pleasing is the pursuit of external approval, and it is fatally flawed. It diverts men from knowing their identity in Christ, shaping them into shifting shams. When a godly man gets caught up in people-pleasing, God-honoring beliefs and values get left behind. This man will eventually compromise on biblical principles that were once nonnegotiable, shying away from even polite confrontations and conflicts that would otherwise strengthen his faith and convictions. Before he knows it, he becomes something he doesn't even recognize: a man whose identity has been shaped by the desires of others.

Proverbs 29:25 serves as a clear caution for men with this struggle: "The fear of man lays a snare, but whoever trusts in the LORD is safe." This verse speaks directly to the challenge faced by those who live to satisfy others. The "fear of man" becomes their driving force, drowning out the voice of God. Consequently, they feel overwhelmed by others' expectations and the dread of being rejected. Their constant craving for approval from others can ensnare them in confusion, exhaustion, and fear. Ultimately, the fear of rejection pushes them to seek fleeting validation from those they are trying so hard to please.

This path clearly contrasts with the way Jesus lived. If you really slow down and read the Gospels, you'll notice the immense pressure Jesus faced to appease the desires of others, particularly the religious leaders of his day. Yet Jesus remained steadfast in prioritizing God's will above human approval. He recognized that listening to and obeying God's commands, even through misunderstanding or rejection, led to fulfillment and purpose. Jesus embraced the unshakable truth that "whoever trusts in the LORD is safe."

REFLECTION AND DISCUSSION QUESTIONS

1. In what areas of your life have you found yourself prioritizing the expectations and desires of others over your own beliefs and values? How has this pursuit of external approval affected your relationship with God and your understanding of your identity in Christ?

2. Considering Jesus's example of prioritizing God's will over human opinions, how can you begin to shift your focus from seeking validation from others to trusting in God's plan for your life? Is there a conflict you fear or a confrontation you need to have to begin taking steps toward pleasing God over man?

THREE | THE VOICE OF THE PAST

The third voice is that of a man's past. It's "the voice of the man you used to be." Many a man has been imprisoned by this one.

All men carry the burden of a sinful past. But some have a wake of sin that is more consequential than others. Their sins are numerous, and the consequences seem to endlessly ripple. Despite the truth that they are new creations, the shadows of their past continue to pursue them, each aftershock a haunting reminder of what they have done. Tragically, there are times when others will use these men's past mistakes as weapons, chaining them to a prison of sin, shame, guilt, and regret. And it's all too common for some men to give the voices of their past undue authority over who they are now.

Yet this is not a voice solely heard by those of us with deeply scarred pasts; it is also familiar to those among us prone to perpetual self-condemnation. For us, this voice surfaces as we lie down at night. Gazing at the ceiling, we revisit the events of our day, and sometimes of our entire lives. Alone with our thoughts, we fixate on our sins and their consequences, projecting them into our future. We hold tightly to these feelings of failure. This voice of guilt punishes our souls. In our minds, we repeatedly tell ourselves:

- » *I'm no good.*
- » *I'm a failure.*
- » *I'm worthless.*
- » *I'm unloved.*

When these guilty thoughts merge with specific memories and intense emotions, we form beliefs and mental images that shape our sense of identity and feelings of worthlessness. They craft a distorted reality about us, one that we ensure to keep hidden from others.

This voice is particularly powerful because of its private and intimate nature. In the end, we come to believe these internal narratives, even though they are unknown and potentially unbelievable to others. We permit this critical voice to dictate our self-worth. Occasionally, we replay these negative thoughts, privately berating ourselves and letting them dictate our behavior and life choices.

Consequently, men who heed this voice often behave in ways that seem irrational, driven by the overwhelming influence of past persistent guilt. This becomes a form of self-imposed penance, a relentless and solitary cycle of personal shame that stubbornly rejects God's intervention in addressing our guilt and shame.

Considering this, Proverbs 28:13 offers incredible insight: "Whoever conceals his transgressions will not prosper, but he who confesses and forsakes them will obtain mercy." This verse directly addresses those afflicted by the voice of the past.

The issue extends beyond the sins, guilt, and continuous self-deception. It's the unconfessed sins and regrets that keep replaying in our minds, amplifying self-criticism. The path to freedom lies in honest confession and rejection of these burdens—the sins, the guilt, the remorse, and the deceitful thoughts—and in placing trust in the freedom from our past through God's grace, mercy, love, and forgiveness, instead of remaining ensnared in a cycle of self-condemnation and shame.

REFLECTION AND DISCUSSION QUESTIONS

1. Reflect on a time when the voice of the past influenced your actions or thoughts. How did the internal narrative of persistent guilt shape your view of yourself? How might confessing and seeking God's grace, mercy, love, and forgiveness alter that perspective?

2. Discuss the impact of unconfessed sins and self-imposed guilt on your spiritual well-being. How can men support each other in breaking the cycle of self-condemnation and embracing God's forgiveness and grace in their daily lives?

FOUR | THE VOICE OF THE PROVEN

Voice four is the voice of the proven man. It's "the voice of the man God says you are." In the end, this is the only voice a man should listen to. It's the voice of the Father of all mankind spoken to his believing sons. It's the one voice that is true and truthful. It's the man God says you are.

Do you know what God says about you?

In Ephesians 1, God reveals an incredible message about who you are in his eyes. He calls you a saint, recognizing your sanctity. He says you're not just blessed, but abundantly so, with every spiritual blessing that comes from above. Think about that—every blessing! You are chosen by God, handpicked for his purpose.

> It's the one voice that is true and truthful. It's the man God says you are.

Ephesians 1 declares that God has adopted you into his family, giving you a place of honor and belonging. In his name, you find redemption, a liberation from all that once held you back. Your past mistakes? Forgiven. Your future? Overflowing with grace. And it's not just a promise. It's a seal, the Holy Spirit marking you as his own. This is a voice of incredible hope that shapes your life.

But Ephesians 1 is just the beginning. Throughout the Old and New Testaments, there are countless promises and truths that speak directly to our hearts and souls. These aren't just words; they are declarations from God himself, penned by godly men, addressed to churches and individuals like us. This is God's voice from heaven, captured in Scripture, proclaiming truth to us about our identity as men of God. It's through these divine words that we understand who we are and to whom we belong.

Do not confuse this with the power of positive thinking, because that kind of self-talk doesn't work. I am not trying to persuade you to think positively about a situation that is not positive. That would be lying to yourself. What I am suggesting is that you preach to yourself the biblical truths about your identity and who God declares you already are in Christ, even while the voices in your head say you're not. That's not positive thinking. That is declaring the truth in the Word of God about you to you.

> **Preach to yourself the biblical truths about your identity. That's not positive thinking. That is declaring the truth in the Word of God about you to you.**

What God says about you is the only truth that a God-fearing man should believe about himself. The other voices are mere nonsense and gibberish. They are aftershocks from the world and echoes from your past. God's voice is the only true and reliable voice.

Knowing this won't change the consequences of your past choices, but it will help you remember God's sovereignty through the consequences. After all, God's voice is greater. It is his voice that spoke creation into existence. God's voice has been echoing across time through all men of renown. God's voice became a living man in Jesus. And this voice remakes and guides men like you and me.

But we must hear his voice and listen to him. God told us this himself, audibly, on the Mount of Transfiguration.

> **This is my beloved Son, with whom I am well pleased; *listen to him*. (Matt. 17:5)**

REFLECTION AND DISCUSSION QUESTIONS

1. In what ways can you discern the voice of God amid the many voices you encounter daily? Reflect on how the truths about your identity in Christ, as mentioned in Ephesians 1, can act as a guide to recognize and prioritize God's voice over others. How do these truths help you distinguish between God's voice and those from the world and echoes from your past?

2. How can you actively apply God's voice to your daily decisions and interactions? Reflect on a recent situation where remembering your identity as a chosen, adopted, and forgiven child of God could have influenced your response or perspective. How can embracing this identity impact your approach to challenges and relationships in your life?

THE WRONG VOICE

Back once again to my story.

I was about twelve and visiting my grandparents one weekend. (This was before I'd moved in with them.) Next door to them lived the grandparents of one of my childhood friends. Adam was adventurous, constantly testing the limits of almost everything. One day, he came over to my grandparents' house with a Daisy Red Ryder BB gun and a brown bag of BBs. We were about as excited as two boys could be. We knew we probably should not have been shooting this rifle off in the backyard, but we could not resist.

We spent about an hour shooting at everything in the backyard: cans, bottles, fence posts, and a couple of birds we missed. But the target that gave us the most pleasurable reward was Grandpa's windchimes. Around the backyard, he had about five metal-pipe windchimes that always sang on windy days. We knew we shouldn't be shooting them, but the reward was such a pleasant sound.

Then Grandpa burst into the backyard through the side gate. He marched over and grabbed the gun from Adam. "Take this thing home," he said sternly, "and don't ever bring it back."

And that was it. The game was up, and the adventure was over.

That was until the next day. No kidding. The next day, Adam came over and said to me, "Want me to go get that rifle again?" (Notice the sound of that devious voice?)

"Of course," I agreed. (Notice how quickly I complied with the voice?) I mean, after all, what boy doesn't want to shoot stuff? But now our mission was even more dangerous. We had to go covert and do it without getting caught by my grandfather. Which I will say made it more fun. (Notice the thrill of the voice of disobedience?)

Five minutes later, we were crawling around the backyard on a mission to assassinate my grandfather's windchimes. This continued for about fifteen minutes until we both started feeling guilty. We discussed it briefly and decided to call it quits.

But I wanted one more shot. I grabbed the gun and cocked it. I turned my back to the windchimes, gestured to Adam, and said confidently, "Watch this."

THE MAN WHO LISTENS

I turned quickly and fired, hoping to hit the chimes. I missed them, but I hit something. We both heard a distinct snap. We waited a few seconds, trying to locate what I had shot. And then we saw it.

Right in the middle of my grandfather's backyard was a PVC water spigot that protruded about one foot out of the ground. I had hit it. At first, it was only dribbling. Then it began spraying a long, narrow stream of water across the yard.

I looked at Adam. He looked at me. Then he grabbed the gun and ran, leaving me to deal with a watery mess.

Now, I had watched a lot of *MacGyver* growing up, so I went to the garage to locate some duct tape. MacGyver fixed everything with duct tape, so I thought I could fix a *white* pipe with *gray* tape that would somehow go unnoticed. By the time I got back out there, the small stream was quickly becoming more aggressive. I started wrapping the pipe with the tape. As I wrapped it, the crack worsened. I frantically wrapped more tape and more tape, but the situation was only getting worse.

Then the pipe split longways. I was now drenched and trying to wrap this entire pipe with a roll of duct tape. I looked up in the window and saw my grandmother drying a dish in the kitchen, shaking her head at me. Then I heard her yell the name that brought the fear of God upon me:

"Grandpa!"

Grandpa calmly came outside. He walked over quietly and stood next to me. He looked at me, taking in that I was soaking wet. Then he looked down at the pipe. He never spoke a word and never changed his expression. He just walked over to the water main, shut it off, and returned to his afternoon session in the recliner inside.

Nothing needed to be said. He had given me a strict command. Instead of listening to his voice, I had listened to another because the pleasure of that voice had beckoned. I learned a hard lesson that day.

This challenge isn't limited to twelve-year-old boys. It's a challenge believing men face every day. The question is, will we listen to the Father's voice, or will we give in to all the others?

> **The question is, will we listen to the Father's voice, or will we give in to all the others?**

Like many men, I've learned to listen to the Father primarily through the pain and consequences of ignoring his voice. We have to learn this way because we don't know how to listen. We've never been taught how to attune to the Father's voice. It's not a skill that's naturally acquired.

So let's learn. Let's learn how to listen to him and tune out the other voices swirling around in our heads.

REFLECTION AND DISCUSSION QUESTIONS

1. In the story, Vince chooses to listen to Adam's voice and the voice of adventure over his grandfather's, leading to disobedience and consequences. This mirrors how we often face temptations in our lives, choosing between right and wrong based on the voices we decide to heed. Reflect on a time when you faced a similar crossroads. What factors influenced your decision? How did the outcome of that decision shape your understanding of listening to God's voice versus the voices of temptation?

2. The challenge of distinguishing between God's voice and the myriad of other voices clamoring for our attention is a common one. Discuss why it's often difficult to tune in to God's voice. What practical steps can you take to better recognize and follow his guidance amid life's distractions? Share a personal experience where you successfully identified and followed God's voice, and describe how it impacted your journey as a man of God.

CULTIVATING MAN'S LISTENING

Our listening lesson begins in the gospel of Mark:

> Again he [Jesus] began to teach beside the sea. And a very large crowd gathered about him, so that he got into a boat and sat in it on the sea, and the whole crowd was beside the sea on the land. And he was teaching them many things in parables, and in his teaching he said to them: "Listen! Behold, a sower went out to sow. And as he sowed, some seed fell along the path, and the birds came and devoured it. Other seed fell on rocky ground, where it did not have much soil, and immediately it sprang up, since it had no depth of soil. And when the sun rose, it was scorched, and since it had no root, it withered away. Other seed fell among thorns, and the thorns grew up and choked it, and it yielded no grain. And other seeds fell into good soil and produced grain, growing up and increasing and yielding thirtyfold and sixtyfold and a hundredfold." And he said, "He who has ears to hear, let him hear." (Mark 4:1-9)

In the first century, when farming was one of the most common occupations, everyday conversations often related to agriculture. The topic provided a rich context for teaching because the principles of farming were transferable to any situation. In this text, Jesus was making abstract spiritual truths accessible to regular people by teaching in a way they could understand.

Jesus's parable was vivid to them, but because most of us in our time are so far removed from agrarian culture, let's ensure we understand these four soils.

THE PATH

For a first-century farmer, the path was a well-trodden, compacted strip of land around the field's boundary. It was the area where farmers and travelers walked, hardening it over time. When Jesus referenced seeds falling on the path, farmers would have instantly understood the impossibility of a seed penetrating this hardened ground. Seeds that fell here would lie on the surface and be exposed to the sun. They became the birds' easiest meals.

THE ROCKY SOIL

The reference to the rocky soil would evoke images of a deceptive layer of soil that looked promising from the surface but concealed an unexposed layer of rock, perhaps limestone, just below the ground. This soil would allow seeds to germinate quickly due to the warmth, but the rock would prevent deep root growth. On a blistering day, the heat would intensify, overheating the hidden stone, which would cook the plant's roots and cause young vegetation to wither and die.

THE THORNY SOIL

Next was the soil full of thorny weeds. Weeds were a persistent threat, then as now, competing with crops for nutrients and sunlight. When Jesus spoke of seeds falling among the thorns, the farmers in his audience would've visualized a patch of soil infested with invasive plants. The presence of these plant pests choked the growth of the good seeds, robbing them of their potential.

THE GOOD SOIL

Good soil is the farmer's dream. Rich, fertile, and free of obstructions, it offers the ideal environment for seeds to thrive. The first-century farmer would've understood that this soil didn't just happen by accident. It required intentional care, cultivation, and hard work. Seeds planted here would not only grow but were also likely to yield an exceptional harvest.

These are the four soils. But remember, Jesus was not giving his listeners a lesson in farming. They already knew how to do that. This was a representative story, called a parable, which Jesus was using to explain something to them: namely, the ways that men listen and the results when they do or don't.

HEARTFELT LISTENING

Even in how Jesus delivered this parable, he performed a teaching hat trick. First, he illustrated listening. Second, he instructed the people to listen. Third, he explained the various ways in which they might listen.

First, Jesus strategically moved his instruction from land to sea. He got into a boat and taught those still on the land. He was using the natural surroundings to his advantage to amplify his voice to increase the audience's capacity to hear. This setting, with the crowd gathered along the shore, maximized the acoustic properties of the area. By doing so, he ensured that his message was heard by the crowd that had gathered along the shore. In this way, Jesus cleverly used nature's own sound system to reach every listener effectively, which was very important, given the subject matter.

Second, he explicitly told them to listen. His message was framed with a clear call to attention. He began with the directive "Listen!" and concluded with the affirmation "He who has ears to hear, let him hear."

Third, he outlined how men listen, which was the core message of the parable. He explained the four distinct ways that men listen to or ignore the truth. Each of the soils corresponded to a way men listen and receive the truth within their hearts.

THE UNRECEPTIVE HEART

The unreceptive heart is characterized as hardened, much like the trodden path in the parable. The constant traffic of life's experiences, perspectives, and perhaps even betrayals has compacted the soil of this man's heart, making it impenetrable. Either way, the seeds of truth don't even get a chance to settle into his heart. They lie exposed and thus rejected.

THE SHALLOW HEART

The man with a shallow heart is passionate and immediately receptive to and captivated by the truth. His heart embraces truth with enthusiasm and the promise of growth. But beneath the surface, there is an unseen competition. His passion never takes deep root. Bring in a few trials—be it financial woes, health concerns, or personal strife—and his enthusiasm withers, exposing a shallow commitment.

THE DIVIDED HEART

Next is the man with a divided heart. Though he does hear and receive the truth, he is surrounded by the voices of other predators—worldly perspectives, social pressures, personal ambitions—that eventually crowd out the voice of God. These "thorns" choke his spiritual growth, preventing production in his life.

THE RECEPTIVE HEART

Finally, the man who has a receptive heart produces the fruitful life Jesus wants us to know. His heart is fertile ground, fully prepared to nurture the seeds of truth. He doesn't just hear the truth; he acts on it, resulting in incredible spiritual growth. His faith produces tangible results, bearing amazing results—enriching his life and the lives of those around him.

The bottom line of this teaching is threefold.

1. Every man in the story hears the truth.
2. Only one man hears and acts on the truth.
3. Only that same man produces fruitful results.

> **If you lack spiritual fruit in your life, you might need to listen better. Become increasingly receptive to God's truth.**

The conclusion is this: if you lack spiritual fruit in your life, you might need to listen better. The good news is that, in this story, Jesus reduced listening to a single understandable principle. If you embrace this principle, you will, by nature, improve your listening.

Become increasingly receptive to God's truth.

That's it. But here's the deal. It's harder to do than you think.

REFLECTION AND DISCUSSION QUESTIONS

1. Which of the four types of hearts or soils (unreceptive, shallow, divided, receptive) do you currently identify with in your spiritual journey? What led you to this identification?

2. What are the key distractions or challenges that prevent you from being a receptive listener to God's truth? How do these challenges affect your daily life and decisions?

3. Reflect on the difference between just hearing the truth and acting on it. Can you recall a recent situation where you acted on God's truth? What were the outcomes?

BECOMING A RECEPTIVE MAN

Back to my story.

Let's fast-forward to about seven years into my marriage. My wife and I were having a major argument.

Frankly, she usually comes out on top of our disagreements. Sure, she might look sweet and gentle, but in a debate, she's fierce, like a lioness. She has this circular way of arguing with me. She makes one point, then shifts to a subpoint, and then another, and yet another. It's like being caught in the spin of a flushing toilet, and I am the one who gets flushed every time.

In the heat of this major dispute, she commented on my character. It felt like a blow below the belt—a total character assassination. I can't even recall what she said now, but the kicker was that, deep down, I knew she was right.

A wave of conviction washed over me. I was exhausted from the back-and-forth and had zero appetite for another lap around the toilet bowl of this no-win situation. Just then, a fleeting thought crossed my mind: *What if I admitted she might be right?*

So I looked her in the eyes and politely said, "You may be right."

Now, before you get too impressed by my courage, I did not say, "You are right." I said, "You *may* be right."

But what happened next surprised me. Her face went pale. For the first time in our battles, she was temporarily thrown off balance. I hadn't seen that coming. The atmosphere was so thick with surprise that I continued. I elaborated on how she might have pinpointed one of my fundamental flaws.

That moment transformed the rest of our marriage from my point of view. More than that, it fundamentally changed me as a man, husband, father, and leader.

What I learned from that experience was invaluable. I realized the significance of being open to hearing and seeing the truth about myself, admitting my faults, and then working to align these imperfections with the truth of God's teachings. I know I'm not the only man out there who isn't skilled at this. Mainly because this type of deep listening requires some digging into the hardened soil of our hearts.

In terms of Jesus's parable, we might say that men often don't listen because their hearts aren't receptive to the truth. Their hearts aren't soft enough yet to receive it and nurture it. They are still resistant in some way and need to till the soil of the heart to become more receptive.

> Be open to hearing and seeing the truth about yourself, admit your faults, then work to align these imperfections with the truth of God's teachings.

Most men who read the Parable of the Sower and Soils assume that the application is merely for four different types of people. But what the parable illustrates are four types of receptivity to the truth. In my opinion, one man can be all four types all the time. He can be radically receptive to the truth on one matter and radically unreceptive on another. I have come to learn that I must work on being receptive in certain areas more than others. Sometimes there is hard soil in a corner of my heart that needs a jackhammer, skid loader, and a team of men with hardhats and pickaxes.

Guess what? You are going to have to do this hard work if you want to be a more productive man. Now let me make some practical suggestions on how to till the soil of your heart if it's still a little hard, rocky, or thorny in some areas.

DO YOU HAVE SOME HARD SOIL?

If you're one of those men with a hardened heart that needs some spading, here are some things you might do:

Start by recognizing how your heart became so resistant to God. It might be good to journal about it or talk it out. Everyone has a hard place. But some of us have a place that's especially hard because we have been through trauma. If you've had to endure the heartbreak of divorce, face the grief of unexpected loss, grapple with the aftereffects of abuse, navigate the psychological toll of war, or struggle with substance abuse, such events will harden you as a man. Over time, they may result in stoicism, and that emotional detachment may form defensive barriers around your heart. (Life hack: sitting down with a trusted Christian counselor will significantly help the process.)

Second, after identifying all of this, you will need to pick away at the problems for a while. Your picking might include resolving your denial and blame, setting new boundaries, and educating yourself. Also, committing this process to God will result in the ground getting more workable even while you're sleeping or are off doing other things.

Third, after a lot of work swinging the pickaxe at this one, there will come a spiritual opportunity—understanding how to communicate your story in a way that it ministers to others. Some of today's greatest ministries have been born out of incredible trauma and pain: DivorceCare, Prison Fellowship, Financial Peace University, Celebrate Recovery, and the like. All of these arose as redemptive acts from men who had worked through their hard-soil moments.

And do you know what this means? It means that even hardened, unreceptive men can find a redemptive and productive use if they do the hard work and dig deep.

So, get to picking.

REFLECTION AND DISCUSSION QUESTIONS

1. What specific events or experiences in your life have contributed to hardening your heart toward God and others?

2. What are some examples of denial or blame in your life that you need to confront to start healing?

3. What are some ways you can use your experiences to create or contribute to a ministry or support group like DivorceCare or Celebrate Recovery?

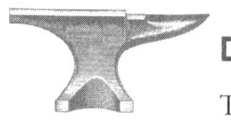

DO YOU HAVE SOME ROCKY SOIL?

The men who contend with shallow, rocky soil in their hearts will have a different process.

If you want to pulverize the layers of rock just below the surface, the first thing you can do is spend time developing basic spiritual disciplines. Men with rocky soil tend to burn fast and hot with enthusiasm but fail to engage in spiritual stabilizers like spiritual disciplines.

Spiritual disciplines are like a slow, deep plow. They move the dirt and expose the rock. Men who burn fast and hot often think they can bypass the slow, deep work of things like daily prayer, daily journaling, and the daily reading of Scripture. They live from one spiritual high to the next and aren't ready for the unexpected lows. But we've got to have more depth than that. You might even have to force yourself to do these things for thirty, sixty, or ninety days before they become habits. But it will pay off.

Second, you need to get a spiritual mentor who has hit the same rocks you keep hitting. Find someone even more stable and steady than you who can mentor you over the coming season. He will help you see and know things you don't yet see or know. Lean on him for guidance and encouragement during moments of doubt or faltering enthusiasm.

Third, join a men's small group and surround yourself with other men who believe in Jesus and read the Bible. A spiritual community will significantly help men like this because it reinforces faith in God in those low times. Essentially, the key to softening the "rocky of heart" is consistency and intentional engagement, ensuring that your faith takes deeper root so the heat of life doesn't burn you out.

So, get going and be steady.

REFLECTION AND DISCUSSION QUESTIONS

1. What specific spiritual disciplines can you implement daily to create more depth in your spiritual life, and what challenges do you anticipate in maintaining them?

2. What qualities should you look for in a spiritual mentor, especially someone who has navigated similar challenges as yours?

3. Reflect on the importance of community in your spiritual life. How does surrounding yourself with others who share your beliefs impact your faith journey?

DO YOU HAVE SOME THORNY SOIL?

If you're a man with thorny soil in your heart, here are some things you might do to deal with the thorns.

First, to become more receptive, you are going to have to intentionally distance yourself from the modern distractions that are competing with your spiritual growth. A practical first step would be initiating a digital detox. The relentless pings and notifications of today's technology can crowd out God's voice. Setting aside dedicated screen-free times or days will create sacred spaces that allow for spiritual clarity.

Second, double down on this by creating a counter rhythm that prioritizes devotional and Bible reading. Set a regular time for this each day. You might prefer the serenity of early mornings or the calm of late evenings. These moments of reflection, prayer, or meditation foster a deeper connection with God and a safeguard against worldly dissonance.

Third, recognize that some thorns come from distractions that are not always self-evident. Set clear boundaries by limiting interactions or environments that consistently derail the spiritual focus that leads to a God-centered life.

Fourth, be sure you're part of a men's group too. One that doesn't always discuss the issues of this world but instead knows how to transcend them. Immersing yourself in Scripture and faith-based discussions will provide spiritual sustenance to navigate the thorny terrains of life, ensuring that the truths of God remain paramount in your heart.

Start detoxing and fill your mind with thoughts that matter.

REFLECTION AND DISCUSSION QUESTIONS

1. What modern distractions most frequently interfere with your ability to focus on your spiritual growth and connection with God?

2. How can establishing a regular routine of reflection, prayer, or meditation strengthen your spiritual life and guard against worldly dissonance?

3. How can you identify and set clear boundaries to limit interactions or environments that derail your spiritual journey?

4. How can being part of a men's group that focuses on transcending worldly issues support your spiritual journey?

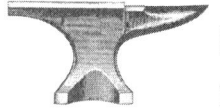

DO YOU HAVE SOME GOOD SOIL?

If you're a man with a heart of good soil, listen closely. Here are some items for you.

First off, guard that harvest with everything you've got. It's easy to think you're set once you've got good soil. But remember, life has a way of throwing curveballs. Be on the lookout for sneaky predators like pride, complacency, and doubt. The voices of distraction, discouragement, temptation, and comparison often whisper to us men, seeking to divert us from our God-given path. While you might be reaping bountifully now, always remember that your heart's soil condition isn't static. Like a diligent farmer, you've got to keep tilling, nurturing, and tending to it. Don't get complacent; the work is never done.

> **Keep tilling, nurturing, and tending to your heart's condition. Don't get complacent; the work is never done.**

Second, you need to lead and disciple others. Trust me, there are brothers out there who are looking at you, thinking, *How does he do it?* They're curious about how you've cultivated that receptive heart and how you consistently tune in and act on God's Word. It's not enough to thrive on your own. Like Jesus, it's your obligation to guide, mentor, and uplift. Share your testimony, your strategies, and your faith journey. By showing them, telling them, and teaching them, you're not just passing on knowledge but also shaping the next generation of men with hearts of good soil. Remember, iron sharpens iron.

So step up, be that beacon, and let's keep building an army of men deeply rooted in faith.

REFLECTION AND DISCUSSION QUESTIONS

1. What specific forms of pride, complacency, or doubt could potentially threaten your current spiritual state?

2. What aspects of your faith journey and practices do you think could most benefit others, and how can you effectively share these with them?

A FINAL CHARGE OF RECEPTIVITY

Regardless of where you find yourself on the spectrum of receptivity, whether your heart is like hardened soil, rocky ground, thorny territory, or fertile soil, there's always room for growth. The journey toward becoming a man of good soil, deeply rooted in faith and receptive to God's truth, is ongoing and transformative.

So, don't settle for mediocrity or complacency. Commit to the hard work of tilling the soil of your heart, removing the obstacles that hinder your receptivity to God's voice, and nurturing a faith that bears abundant fruit. Whether it's through confronting past traumas, developing spiritual disciplines, disconnecting from distractions, or sharing your faith journey with others, each step you take brings you closer to embodying the qualities of good soil.

And remember, the impact of your receptivity goes far beyond your own life. As you cultivate a heart that is open to God's truth, you become a beacon of hope and transformation for those around you—like my grandfather was for me. So, embrace the challenge, lean into the process, and let's build better men of God together.

Our time desperately needs more men of good soil—men who are forged in deep-rooted faith and radiate God's love, wisdom, and strength. When one man's heart becomes good soil, it has the potential to nourish countless others.

> **When one man's heart becomes good soil, it has the potential to nourish countless others.**

THE NEXT BOOK

As we close the pages of *Essential Elements: Forging Godly Men*, we look back and recall that we've walked together through a powerful journey. We started by uncovering the molten core of true manhood, boldly confronting our sins and looking to Jesus, the ultimate model of manhood. We've embraced repentance and discovered the transformative power of listening. This journey has been about more than just understanding; it's been about changing and growing. This is the foundation.

But, brother, this is not where our path ends. It's merely a starting point to something even deeper and more challenging.

In our next adventure, *The Blacksmith's Discipline: Honing Godly Men*, we're going to stoke our spiritual fires higher. We'll learn how *prayer*, like the bellows in a blacksmith's forge, breathes life and intensity into our faith. We'll dive into *Scripture*, our blueprint guiding every precise strike we make in life. We'll also talk about the ironclad bonds of *brotherhood* and how they sharpen us, and we'll explore the meticulous skill of living a life of *accountability*. It's about refining our character, one day at a time, with God's precision. And finally, we'll look at how serving others through our *ministry* shapes us just as much as it shapes the world around us. Each discipline is not just a tool for self-improvement; it's a tool for forging a deeper bond with God.

So, as you turn to book two, keep living out the lessons from book one. Let these truths be the anvil on which we forge our lives. The journey to become men of God is ongoing, and the forge is calling us back. Let's step into it together, continuing to grow as warriors for Christ.

STRONG AS A MAN OF GOD

With Scripture, prayers, and actionable ideas, this devotional series from Bible teacher Vince Miller challenges you to stand up for your faith and draw closer to God. Each devotion reminds you that even in the hard moments and the stressful days, God is with you to strengthen, help, and provide.

Available from David C Cook
and everywhere books are sold

DAVID C COOK
transforming lives together